CONDENSED
CHAOS

CONDENSED CHAOS

An Introduction to Chaos Magic

by
Phil Hine

Foreword by
Peter J. Carroll

NEW FALCON PUBLICATIONS
TEMPE, ARIZONA, U.S.A.

International Standard Book Number: 1-56184-117-X
Library of Congress Catalog Card Number: 94-69291

First Edition 1995
Second Printing 1996 • Third Printing 1999
Fourth Printing 2003 • Fifth Printing 2004
Sixth Printing 2005 • Seventh Printing 2006
Eighth Printing 2007

The author may be reached by writing to:
Phil Hine, c/o BM Coyote
London WC1N 3XX, England

Book design by Nicholas Tharcher
Cover design by S. Jason Black

The paper used in this publication meets the minimum requirements of the American National Standard for Permanence of Paper for Printed Library Materials Z39.48-1984

Address all inquiries to:

email: info@newfalcon.com
website: http://www.newfalcon.com
NEW FALCON PUBLICATIONS
1753 East Broadway Road #101-277
Tempe, AZ 85282 U.S.A.

(or)

320 East Charleston Blvd. #204-286
Las Vegas, NV 89104 U.S.A.

With thanks to
Christopher Hyatt,
Robert & Stephanie Williams,
Ian Read,
Ed Wallis,
Hannibal the Cannibal,
Vishvanath,
Maria Strutz,
Barry Walker
and
Rodney Orpheus

Table of Contents

Foreword

by Pete Carroll

The paradigm shift now occurring at the cutting edge of magic has many roots. The symbolic syncretism of the Golden Dawn a century ago, which fused renaissance Hermeticism with oriental esoterics drawn from the European imperial experience, only fully flowered when Aleister Crowley added a battery of gnostic power techniques culled from diverse cultural sources. Then along came Austin Spare, who identified the basic sleight of mind techniques underlying all forms of magic, and showed us that we could treat the whole baroque symbolism of magic as entirely optional. Spare invented the Postmodernist approach to magic well before the cultural advent of Existentialism or Postmodernism.

The theories of Special and General Relativity added little to esoteric theory although the idea of cultural relativism manifested in syncretic occultism long before it found general social acceptance. However, that other main pillar of twentieth century science, Quantum Physics, provides enormous support for many areas of metaphysical theory and, indeed, suggests considerable scope for its extension. So far, only Chaos Magic seems to have welcomed it on board. Shortly after the launch of the Chaos Magic paradigm, Chaos Mathematics developed from Catastrophe Theory and confirmed the Chaoist hypothesis that some mechanism must exit to scale up subatomic indeterminacy into the macroscopic world of our experience.

So much of what magicians have taken for granted this century stems from the work of the Golden Dawn and Aleister Crowley. Much of what will constitute standard magical theory and practice in the next century will derive from the state-of-the-art ideas and techniques currently under development in Chaos Magic. This book, by a rising star of the new tradition, represents an outstanding contribution to the revolution now occurring.

9

CHAPTER ONE

IS CHAOS MAGIC?

WHAT IS MAGIC?

The world is magical; we might get a sense of this after climbing a mountain and looking down upon the landscape below, or in the quiet satisfaction at the end of one of those days when everything has gone right for us. Magic is a doorway through which we step into mystery, wildness, and immanence. We live in a world subject to extensive and seemingly, all-embracing systems of social and personal control that continually feed us the lie that we are each alone, helpless, and powerless to effect change. Magic is about change. Changing your circumstances so that you strive to live according to a developing sense of personal responsibility; that you can effect change around you if you choose; that we are not helpless cogs in some clockwork universe. All acts of personal/collective liberation are magical acts. Magic leads us into exhilaration and ecstasy; into insight and understanding; into changing ourselves and the world in which we participate. Through magic we may come to explore the possibilities of freedom.

Surely this is simple enough? But no, magic has become obfuscated under a weight of words, a welter of technical terms which exclude the uninitiated and serve those who are eager for a 'scientific' jargon with which to legitimise their enterprise into something self-important and pompous. Abstract spiritual spaces have been created in the midst of which tower the Babel-like Lego constructions of 'inner planes', spiritual hierarchies and 'occult truths' which forget that the world around us is magical. The mysterious has been misplaced. We search through dead languages and tombs for 'secret knowledge', ignoring the mystery of life that is all around us. So for the moment, forget what you've read about spiritual enlightenment, becoming a 99th level Magus and impressing your friends with high-flown gobbledygook. Magic is surprisingly simple. What can it offer?

1. A means to disentangle yourself from the attitudes and restrictions you were brought up with and which define the limits of what you may become.

2. Ways to examine your life to look for, understand and modify behavior, emotional and thought patterns which hinder learning and growth.

3. Increase of confidence and personal charisma.

4. A widening of your perception of just what is possible, once you set heart and mind on it.

5. To develop personal abilities, skills and perceptions—the more we see the world, the more we appreciate that it is alive.

6. To have fun. Magic should be enjoyed.

7. To bring about change—in accordance with will.

Magic can do all this, and more. It is an approach to life which begins at the most basic premises—what do I need to survive?—how do I want to live?—who do I want to be?—and then gives a set of conceptual weapons and techniques for achieving those aims.

WHAT IS CHAOS MAGIC?

What do you think of when you hear the word "Chaos?"

— *"A state of things in which chance is supreme"*
— *"An unorganised state of primordial matter before the creation"*
— *"A confused state or mass"*
— *"Chaos was the primal source, first of all"*
— *"This isn't anarchy, this is Chaos"*
— *"In the beginning, there was only Chaos"*
— *"Agents of Chaos cast burning glances at anything or anyone capable of bearing witness to their condition…"*
— *"One must have Chaos in one to give birth to a dancing star"*
— *"Matter is illusion, solidity is illusion, we are illusion. Only Chaos is real"*
— *"In the limitless heavens, shines the countenance of Chaos"*

Chaos is all this and more. A term which means something different for everyone, none of us can ignore Chaos. Over the last twenty years or so, Chaos has become the buzzword of a revolution in thought and method, spawning a new form of science, new technologies; a whole new emerging world-view. While Chaos Theory has been generating debate within the scientific community, Chaos Magic has been creating controversy within occult circles. It has been labeled variously as "English Thelema", "the blackest form of dark power" and "git 'ard magic". At the core of this revolution is the recognition that the scientific world-view which has set the limitations of acknowledged human experience is crumbling, that new visions and models are required, as are new ways of being, and more importantly, new ways of *doing*. Chaos Magic is a new approach to "doing" magic.

CORE PRINCIPLES OF CHAOS MAGIC

While magical systems usually base themselves around a model or map of the spiritual/physical universe, such as the Tree of Life (which can sometimes be described as a Cosmic Filofax), Chaos Magic is based on a very few 'Core Principles' which generally underlie its approach to magic (they are not universal axioms however, so feel free to swap 'em around).

1. *The Avoidance of Dogmatism*. Chaos Magicians strive to avoid falling into dogmatism (unless expressing dogmatism is part of a temporary belief system they have entered). Discordians use 'Catmas' such as "Us Discordians must stick apart!" Thus Chaos Magicians feel entitled to change their minds, contradict themselves and come up with arguments that are alternatively plausible and implausible. It has been pointed out that we invest a lot of time and energy in being right. What's wrong with being wrong occasionally?

2. *Personal Experience* is paramount. In other words, don't take my word that such-and-such is the case, check it out for yourself. Magic has suffered extensively from 'armchair theorists' who have perpetuated myths and out-of-date information purely due to laziness of one kind or another. Sometimes it's interesting to ask awkward questions just to see what the self-appointed experts come out with. Some will emit a stream of verbal diarrhea rather than admit to not knowing the answer, whereas a true adept will probably say "I haven't a f*****g clue." Quite early on, Chaos Magicians came to the startling

discovery that once you strip away the layers of dogma, personal beliefs, attitudes and anecdotes around any particular technique of practical magic, it can be quite simply described.

3. *Technical Excellence*. One of the early misconceptions about Chaos Magic was that it gave practitioners carte blanche to do whatever they liked, and so become sloppy (or worse, soggy) in their attitudes to self-assessment, analysis, etc. Not so. The Chaos approach has always advocated rigorous self-assessment and analysis, emphasised practice at what techniques you're experimenting with until you get the results that you desire. Learning to 'do' magic requires that you develop a set of skills and abilities and if you're going to get involved in all this weird stuff, why not do it to the best of your ability?

4. *Deconditioning*. The Chaos paradigm proposes that one of the primary tasks of the aspiring magician is to thoroughly decondition hirself from the mesh of beliefs, attitudes and fictions about self, society, and the world. Our ego is a fiction of stable self-hood which maintains itself by perpetuating the distinctions of 'what I am/what I am not, what I like/what I don't like', beliefs about ones politics, religion, gender preference, degree of free will, race, subculture etc. all help maintain a stable sense of self, while the little ways in which we pull against this very stability allows us to feel as though we are unique individuals. Using deconditioning exercises, we can start to widen the cracks in our consensual reality which hopefully, enables us to become less attached to our beliefs and ego-fictions, and thus able to discard or modify them when appropriate.

5. *Diverse Approaches*. As mentioned earlier, 'traditional' approaches to magic involve choosing one particular system and sticking to it. The Chaos perspective, if nothing else, encourages an eclectic approach to development, and Chaos Magicians are free to choose from any available magical system, themes from literature, television, religions, cults, parapsychology, etc. This approach means that if you approach two Chaos Magicians and ask 'em what they're doing at any one moment, you're rarely likely to find much of a consensus of approach. This makes Chaos difficult to pin down as one thing or another, which again tends to worry those who need approaches to magic to be neatly labeled and clear.

6. *Gnosis*. One of the keys to magical ability is the ability to enter Altered States of Consciousness at will. We tend to draw a distinct line between 'ordinary consciousness' and 'altered states', where in fact we move between different states of consciousness—such as daydreams, 'autopilot' (where we carry out actions without cognition) and varying degrees of attention, all the time. However, as far as magic is concerned, the willed entry into intense altered states can be divided into two poles of 'Physiological Gnosis'—Inhibitory states, and Excitatory states. The former includes physically 'passive' techniques such as meditation, yoga, scrying, contemplation and sensory deprivation while the latter includes chanting, drumming, dance, emotional and sexual arousal.

A BRIEF HISTORY OF CHAOS

The Chaos Magic movement had its first stirrings in the late nineteen seventies, in England. While the new phenomena of punk rock was grabbing the newspaper headlines, and scientists across the world were beginning to delve into the mysterious mathematical world of fractals and non-linear dynamics, a new approach to magical practice was being synthesized in the wilds of West Yorkshire. At the time, English occultism was very much dominated by the three strands of popular Witchcraft, Western Qabalah, and Thelema. At least, there were enough people interested in these approaches to spawn supporting magazines. In one such magazine, *The New Equinox*, there appeared the early writings of Peter J. Carroll, who is considered the foremost exponent of modern Chaos Magic. By 1978, there appeared the first advertisements for the "Illuminates of Thanateros", an order who's practices were composed of a blend of shamanism, Taoism, Tantra and Thelema. The announcement of this new order was shortly followed by the first edition of Peter Carroll's *Liber Null,* which while describing the basic philosophy and practical approaches, did not contain the term 'Chaos Magic'. *Liber Null* was closely followed by *The Book of Results* by Ray Sherwin, which lucidly explained Austin Osman Spare's great magical innovation—sigil magic. Austin Osman Spare is considered by many to be the "grandfather" of Chaos Magic. An obscure figure, brought to light by the work of Kenneth Grant, Spare was a superb magical artist, sorcerer, and spiritualist. At a time when many of his contemporaries sneered at table-tapping and contacting 'spirit guides' in favour of elaborate Rosicrucian ceremonies, Spare was painting the spirits he was in contact with, and using his own system of 'sentient letters'—sigils—to manifest his desires. Spare was not particularly enamoured of the Golden Dawn-style approach to magic, and makes some very acid comments on the subject in *The Book of Pleasure* (1913).

The *Book of Pleasure* (subtitled: *The Psychology of Ecstasy*) contains the essentials of Spare's magical philosophy, and the key techniques with which he applied it. It is not an easy book to read, and Spare is often referred to as an "incomprehensible mystic." His vocabulary is wide, his use of grammar is strange, and he uses many terms in ways that give them a different meaning from their usual context. Nor was he attempting to write in a "textbook" style that modern readers are used to, and *The Book of Pleasure* is very stylistically reminiscent of an old Grimoire before it has been tidied up. Fortunately, *The Book of Results* gave a very clear exposition of sigil magic, and *Liber Null* also dealt with Spare's concept of the alphabet of desire. Another powerful influence of the development of Chaos Magic was the work of Aleister Crowley. Crowley synthesised a magical world-view—a psychocosm—out of his studies in magical and esoteric fields such as the Golden Dawn, Yoga, Alchemy, Kabalah, and from his experience in other disciplines. Moreover, it is Crowley's life, rather than his voluminous magical and mystical writings that is of interest. Crowley took his personal experience, magical and otherwise, and created his own enclave, beyond the boundaries of conventional morality. He deliberately sought extremes of experience, concealing, and at the same time, revealing himself through a series of colourful personalities. Part of Crowley's attraction for the modern magician is that he created something which has enduring power—a psychocosm which continues to be developed and twisted into different forms. Crowley did not so much 'follow' a tradition, he *embodied* a dynamic process of reality engagement—creating his own path from whatever he happened to find in front of him.

The early growth of Chaos Magic was characterised by a loose network of informal groups who came together to experiment with the possibilities of the new current. With the demise of The New Equinox, the 'chaos kids' reported their results and heresies in the pages of a new British Occult magazine, *The Lamp of Thoth*. The early Chaos books were joined by two tapes 'The Chaos Concept' which discussed the basics of Chaos Magic, and 'The Chaochamber', a science-fiction Pathworking which combined elements of *Star Trek*, Michael Moorcock, and H. G. Wells. The Sorcerer's Apprentice Press then re-released *Liber Null* and *The Book of Results,* as well as Pete Carroll's *Psychonaut.* These, together with articles from the growing Chaos corpus in *The Lamp of Thoth*, drew more people into experimenting with the new approach. Thanks to the efforts of Ralph Tegtmeier, the Chaos approach was also receiving attention in continental Europe.

The simple message of Chaos Magic is that, what is fundamental to magic is the actual *doing* of it—that like sex, no amount of theorising and intellectualisation can substitute for the actual experience. Carroll's *Liber Null*, therefore, presented the bare bones of the magical techniques which can be employed to bring about change in one's circumstances. *Liber Null* concentrated on techniques, saying that the actual methods of magic are basically shared by the different systems, despite the differing symbols, beliefs and dogmas. What symbol systems you wish to employ is a matter of choice, and that the webs of belief which surround them are means to an end, rather than ends in themselves (more on this later).

An important influence on the development of Chaos Magic was the writing of Robert Anton Wilson and Company, particularly the Discordian Society who revered Eris, the Greek goddess of Chaos. The Discordians pointed out that humour, clowning about and general light-heartedness was conspicuously absent from magic, which had a tendency to become very 'serious and self-important'. There was (and to a certain extent remains) a tendency for occultists to think of themselves as an initiated 'elite' compared to the rest of humanity. The Discordian Society is, in its own words "...a tribe of philosophers, theologians, magicians, scientists, artists, clowns, and similar maniacs who are intrigued with ERIS GODDESS OF CONFUSION and with Her doings." The existence of the Discordian Society was first popularised in Robert Anton Wilson and Robert Shea's blockbusting *Illuminatus!* trilogy, and also in Malaclypse The Younger's book *Principia Discordia* which sets out the basic principles of the Discordian Religion—a religion based around the Greek Goddess, Eris.

Traditionally, Eris was a daughter of Nox (night) and the wife of Chronus. She begat a whole bunch of Gods—Sorrow, Forgetfulness, Hunger, Disease, Combat, Murder, Lies—nice kids! The ancient Greeks attributed any kind of upset or discord to her. With the fall of the ancient empires, Eris disappeared, though it is suspected that she had a hand in 'manifesting' the first bureaucracies, triplicate forms, and insurance companies. She didn't put in a personal appearance again on spaceship Gaia again until the late 1950's, when she appeared to two young Californians, who later became known as Omar Ravenhurst and Malaclypse The Younger. Eris appointed them the "Keepers of the Sacred Chao" and gave them the message to: "Tell constricted mankind that there are no rules, unless they choose to invent rules." After which Omar and Mal appointed each other High Priest of his own madness, and declared themselves each to be a Society of Discordia, whatever that may be. Eris has since climbed her way from historical footnote to mythic mega-star, and the Discordian Movement, if such a thing can be said to exist, is growing on both sides of the Atlantic, helped by the Discordian tactic of declaring that everyone is a genuine Pope. More people are getting into the idea of a religion based on the celebration of confusion and madness. The central Greek myth that Eris figures prominently in is the ever-continuing soap opera of 'Mount Olympus—Home of the Gods'; the episode which inadvertently brought about the Trojan War. It seems that Zeus was throwing a party and did not want to invite Eris because of her reputation as a trouble-maker. Infuriated by the snub, Eris fashioned a golden apple inscribed with the word Kallisti, ("to the prettiest one") and tossed it into the hall where all the guests were. Three of the invited Goddesses, Athena, Hera, and Aphrodite, each claimed the apple for themselves and started fighting and throwing food around. To settle the dispute, Zeus ordered all three to submit to the judgement of a mortal over just who was 'the prettiest one', and said mortal was Paris, son of the King of Troy. Zeus sent all three to Paris, via Hermes, but each Goddess tried to outwit the others by sneaking out early and offering a bribe to Paris. Athena offered Paris victory in battle, Hera, great wealth, while Aphrodite 'merely loosened the clasps by which her tunic was fastened and unknotted her girdle,' also offering Paris the most beautiful of mortal women. So, Aphrodite got the apple, and Paris got off with Helen, who unfortunately happened to be married to Menelaus, King of Sparta. Thanks to the meddling of Athena and Hera, the Trojan war followed and the rest, as they say, is history.

Nowadays, in our more chaos-positive age, Eris has mellowed somewhat, and modern Discordians associate her with all intrusions of 'weirdness' in their lives, from synchronous to mischievous occurrences, creative flashes of inspiration, and wild parties. She does get a little bitchy at times, but who doesn't? It was the Discordians that pointed out that amidst the long list of dualisms that occultists were fond of using, the opposites of humour/seriousness had been left aside. Humour is important in magic. As a colleague of mine once said, we're too important to take ourselves seriously. Some members of the I.O.T. Pact, for example, use Laughter as a form of banishing, and of course there is nothing like laughter to deflate the pompous, self-important occult windbags that one runs into from time to time. *Important*: rituals, when silly, can be no less effective than when you keep a straight face. Magic is fun—otherwise, why do it?

Unlike the variety of magical systems which are all based in some mythical or historically-derived past (such as Atlantis, Lemuria, Albion, etc.), Chaos Magic borrows freely from Science Fiction, Quantum Physics, and anything else its practitioners choose to. Rather than trying to recover and maintain a tradition that links back to the past (and former glories), Chaos Magic is an approach that enables the individual to use anything that s/he thinks is suitable as a temporary belief or symbol system. What matters is the results you get, not the 'authenticity' of the system used. So Chaos Magic then, is not a system—it utilises systems and encourages adherents to devise their own, giving magic a truly Postmodernist flavour.

Needless to say, Chaos Magic quickly began to acquire a 'sinister' reputation. This was due to three factors; firstly that its "pick'n'mix/D.I.Y" approach to magic was frowned upon by the 'traditionalist' schools, secondly that many people associated chaos with 'anarchy' and other negative associations, and thirdly that some Chaos Magic publications were hyped as being 'blasphemous, sinister, and dangerous' in a way that they were not, which proved all the same to be an attractive glamour for those who required such a boost to the ego. Although there were Satanic orders around at the time of Chaos Magic's early promotion, they certainly did not promulgate themselves as visibly as other occult groups. Chaos Magic was thus both attractive for those people looking for a "dark" glamour to become involved with and equally, those who needed a "satanic opponent" to bolster up their fantasies of being "whiter-than-white."

What is notable concerning the growth of Chaos Magic is that from its beginnings, it has been very much perceived as "experimental" magic. This means not only experimenting with magical techniques and practices, but also questioning and testing a great many of the concepts which many people who become involve in the occult accept as implicitly 'true'. The late nineteen-eighties gave rise to the second great surge of interest in Chaos Magic, with the rise of specialist occult magazines such as *Chaos International* in which practising Chaos Magicians made their technical and philosophical findings known to their peers. This period was one of a great surge of interest in occultism, with the availability of affordable Desktop Publishing systems leading to a surge of self-publishing and special-interest occult magazines being a contributing factor. The diversification of esoteric studies into separate (and almost mutually exclusive) fields continued, and the late eighties also gave rise to the mushrooming of interest in shamanism of one type or another. An important (but often overlooked) element of growing occult movements is the availability of information in the public domain. If you go into any bookstore catering to occult interests, there is likely to be a wide range of titles catering to virtually any subject, from Astrology to Zen. Chaos Magic has not, so far, reached such a high level of visibility. Instead, the ideas have spread by word of mouth, through the information-highways of Internet and Compuserve, through limited edition books and specialist magazines. In a subculture where commercial trends tend to create the illusion of 'separate' occult traditions and approaches, Chaos Magic texts represent the move towards diversity of approach and fluidity of movement between the colour-coded zones of the occult belief-market.

The development of Chaos science and Chaos Magic do go hand in hand, with uncanny (or fortuitous) synchronicities; for example, in 1987 the University of Leeds, England hosted an exhibition of the scientific possibilities of Chaos. Later that year, Leeds was the venue of the first ever "Symposium of Chaos Magic" and, around this period, appeared to be a centre of Chaos Magic activity, with groups such as the aforementioned I.O.T., the 'Circle of Chaos' and 'Leeds Order of Neuromancers' operating around the city.

In a very magical way, 'Chaos' has become fashionable—the buzzword of the Nineties. Fractal designs have crawled their way from computer screens onto t-shirts, rave posters and postcards. The chaos science of non-linear dynamics is now used in fields as diverse as economics to linguistics and has been widely popularised through the character of Ian Malcolm in Spielberg's *Jurassic Park*. It is somehow appropriate that, just as the rise of personal computers assisted the paradigm breakthroughs which allowed chaos science to emerge, so the practical application of chaos formula has led to improvements in computer development—from the use of fractals to model three-dimensional landscapes to fractal-based data compression formula. At a very basic level, Chaos challenges the way in which we habitually experience the world.

FRACTAL LOGIC

If anything, the fractal has become both the main motif of the emerging sciences—both a demonstration of its principles and at the same time an image of popular culture. The staggering beauty and complexity of images such as the Mandelbrot set arises from the application of a simple rule $(x+x2+c)$. The term 'fractal' means self-similar at any scale. When you look into a fractal form, you see variations on the overall shape of the set, no matter how much you increase the scale. It seems that the deeper into the image you go, the more there is to see. Everything is connected to everything else in the set. This similarity can also be seen in natural phenomena such as mountains, clouds, and coastlines. It can be seen to occur in the shape of molecules and galaxies. The fractal is fast becoming one of the most powerful metaphors for explaining and understanding the world. Consciousness can be modeled as having a fractal nature. Certainly much of our learning arises in our minds in the same way that a fractal is modeled on a computer screen. The processes of creative thinking constitute one example. We have isolated ideas, and gradually the relationships between ideas and concepts grow, until we suddenly perceive the 'shape' of a new idea. The ways in which we look into something affects the possibilities of what we will find. If one's learning or attention is broad, rather than narrowly focused and specialised, then one will see the similarity of ideas across different disciplines and specialisations. Also, similar ideas crop up in different cultures, at various points in history. In some ways, the Fractal is a twentieth-century icon of the idea that all things are, at some level, interconnected at any given moment. Chaos Theory is itself a multi-disciplinary theory. It is being applied in a wide diversity of fields, from the study of epilepsy to the fluctuation of stock market prices. In some ways, Chaos Theory's most striking implications concern our implicit experience of the world at a day-to-day level. We have come to accept as 'natural' that events happen in a logical, linear sequence, and that anything which happens outside of this sequence is somehow outside of the natural order of things. This linearity is portrayed in everything from mathematics to popular fiction, to the level where it is *embedded* in our consciousness and taken for granted. It is the way that we tend to think about our experience of the world, but it is not necessarily *how* we really experience the world. Chaos Theory, in a way, points out the obvious: that one event can change those that follow in a way that can have a tremendous impact upon us. We tend to think of ourselves, for example, as being fairly constant day after day, only changing over a span of time. Chaos Theory shows us the complexity which underlies the apparent simplicity. Look at how we model conscious awareness. We talk about 'normal' consciousness and that which is distinct from it as 'Altered States of Consciousness.' Yet we continually shift from one condition of awareness to another; moving in and out from being aware of what is going on around us, a flash of memory, a dash of fantasy, giving attention to a piece of inner dialogue, a loop of song fragment or advertising jingle, daydreaming, wondering about possible futures that we are moving into, and more. When you consider that at any given moment, your consciousness can be engaged in many directions at once, the idea of 'normal consciousness' that we all talk about becomes something of a facade. Consciousness behaves in an analogue (gradual) fashion, not like something definite.

The power of Chaos Theory as a model is that it can approximately model a wide variety of phenomena that previous theories could not. Pre-Chaos science approached phenomena in terms of isolating one element of an event or situation and studying it. For example, the dominant approach to understanding our senses is to study each sense in isolation of the others. This can tell us a lot about each sense, but it is not an accurate way of describing how we experience our senses. It is a very common human tendency to confuse the map with the territory, that is, to act as though the models we use to interpret experience actually are the experience. One of the points that Chaos Theory makes is that no model can describe something utterly accurately—we can only make approximations. Much has been made of Heisenberg's Uncertainty Principle, which demonstrates this concept at a mathematical level.

A version of the Uncertainty Principle which has become a watchword for Chaos Magicians is that famous phrase, attributed to Hassan I Sabbah, that *Nothing Is True, Everything is Permitted.* If "Nothing is True", then questions of 'proof' become irrelevant, and the responsibility—"Permission" for one's actions and beliefs is thrown back upon the individual. If "Nothing is True", then everything becomes art, play, or make-believe. So you can choose your beliefs and attitudes without feeling the necessity of validating them as "Truth" or scientifically valid. Again, this is a rather obvious statement, although it seems that we tend to agree to act as though the situation was otherwise. Single "Truths" which have an essential character, can only be maintained by rigorously ignoring anything which does not conform to a particular belief-system. Thus beliefs survive, even if there is a relative absence of evidence to support them. Chaos Magic recognises the power and malleability of belief, and consequently uses belief as a tool for magical action. That we can quickly allow beliefs to form the bedrock of our interpretation of reality allows us to manipulate the ability for magical purposes.

MAGICAL MODELS

The way that magic is generally conceptualised changes as general paradigm shifts in thinking occur. Until fairly recently (in a broad historical sense), practitioners of magic subscribed to the 'Spirit' Model of Magic, which basically states that the Otherworlds are real, and are inhabited by various pantheons of discrete entities—elementals, demons, angels, goddesses, gods, etc. The task of the magician or shaman is to develop (or inherit) a route map of the Otherworld—to know the short-cuts, and make a few friends (or contact relatives) over there. Having done this, they have to interact with these spirits in a given way, to get them to execute your will. So clergymen pray, shamans stuff sacred mushrooms into their orifices in order to meet their ancestors, while demonologists threaten entities into submission by thundering out bits of the Old Testament.

By the Eighteenth Century, and the rise of Science, the idea of 'Animal Magnetism' arose in the West, the first manifestation of the 'Energy' Model of magic. This model places emphasis on the presence of 'subtle energies' which can be manipulated via a number of techniques. Along came Bulwer Lytton and his idea of 'Vril' energy, Eliphas Levi and the Astral Light, Mediums and ectoplasm, Westernised 'popular' accounts of Prana, Chakras, and Kundalini, and eventually, Wilhelm Reich's Orgone energy.

The next development came with the popularisation of Psychology, mainly due to the Psychoanalytic fads of Freud, Jung and company. During this phase, the Otherworlds became the Innerworlds, demons were rehoused into the Unconscious Mind, and Hidden Masters revealed as manifestations of the 'Higher Self'. For some later exponents of this model, Tarot cards were switched from being a magical-divinatory system to being 'tools' for personal transformation, just as the goddesses/gods came to be seen as not 'real' entities, but psychological symbols or archetypes.

The current up-and-coming paradigm is the 'Cybernetic' model, as we swing into being an information-based culture. This model says that the Universe, despite appearances, is stochastic in nature. Magic is a set of techniques for rousing a neurological storm in the brain which brings about microscopic fluctuations in the Universe, which lead eventually to macroscopic changes—in accordance with the magician's intent.

See Chaos Science, the Butterfly Effect, and all that. Another manifestation of the Cybernetic Model coming to the fore is the new age assertion that crystals work 'just like' computer chips. There are signs that the Cybernetic Model dovetails back into the spirit model, and once you get past the mathematical proofs and weird jargon, the model does display a simple elegance.

Each model has its own attractive glamour, with exponents or opponents on either side. Many occult textbooks contain elements of the Spirit, Energy, and Psychological models quite happily. Should you ever find yourself in the position of having to 'explain' all this weird stuff to an non-aficionado or skeptic, then the Psychological model is probably your best bet. These days, people who ascribe to the Spirit model (if they are not of a Pagan or Occult persuasion themselves), tend to think that they have an exclusive copyright over the use of Spirits! If the person is a computer buff or Fractal phreak, then by all means go for the 'cyberpunk' paradigm. Scientists only tend to accept something if a scientific 'rationale' can be wheeled up. Acupuncture, for example, was until recently explained using the Energy Model, and poo-poohed by the scientific establishment until someone came up with Endorphin stimulation. Now most hospital physio- therapy departments have a set of needles.

While some magicians tend to stick to one favourite model, it is useful to shift among them as the situation befits. Some models have a stronger 'explaining' power and account for some aspects of magic 'better' than others. The Spirit model, by far the oldest, can account for just about any aspect of magic. The Psychological model, while being useful for looking at magic as a process for personal development, has difficulty with situations such as tribal shamans cursing Westerners who (a) don't believe in magic, (b) didn't see the shaman squinting at them, (c) and break out in hives anyway. If you use only one magical model, sooner or later the Universe will present you with something that won't fit your parameters. When you are spending more time defending your models than modifying them, then you know it's time for another spot of deconditioning...report to Room 101.

CHAPTER TWO

MAGIC IN THE MATERIAL WORLD

The 19th Century revivalists of Magic have bequeathed to us, their 'magical children', a false dichotomy of High magic and Low Magic. High magic is about becoming more 'spiritual', and Low Magic, or Sorcery, is merely the manipulation of the mundane, material world. The philosophical roots of this dichotomy lie in post-Enlightenment Christianity; wherein a wedge was driven between the Spiritual (the domain of the Church) and the Temporal (the playground of the emerging Scientists). The occult revivals of the last century sought to reconcile the spiritual yearning with the new power of science, while the power of orthodox religion melted in the flames of war, rapid social change, and the rise of technology. Oddly enough, it is science itself, once the enemy of the spiritual impulse, which now offers reconciliation. The revolutions of Quantum Physics and Non-Linear Dynamics are now returning us to the awareness, long hidden, that the world is magical. That we are, as Alan Moore so eloquently put it *unpredictable beyond the dreams of Heisenberg.* The 'Traditional' High Magicians created towering edifices in abstract space, which they used to climb towards their idea of 'Godhead', seeking transcendence from the embrace of the material world. A few notables amongst these architects of the Spirit have spectacularly fallen from the heights they scaled, and biographers have provided us with neat encapsulations of their blazing passions, while legions of clerkish scribblers still present us with the gleanings of their visions, their notations, and systems. But their time has passed. Magic is no longer the domain of the wealthy, and we need no utterances from rebel angels to announce the uncertainty of the future. Although it is ever the folly of the young to sneer at the mistakes of their forebears, let us not forget that, in essence, their magics worked; that we are here. Even now, I feel the stirrings of the next generation of magi, and it is my fervent hope that they too will surpass the present generation; that they will not be seduced by the past, but will take magic forwards.

Just as the transcendental emphasis of the 19th century magi reflected the driving passions of their age, so too does contemporary magic show up the dominant characteristics of this latter end of the 20th Century: a faith in Technology and a magpie's view of culture. In any of our Western cities, we can daily experience the cultural melting pot of styles from anywhere in the world, from any place or time. So too, we see the tendency to reduce magic to a profusion of techniques, as the would-be magi increasingly search for 'better' techniques; quicker results; instant enlightenments. The present technologists of the spirit run the same risks as the previous generations' architects of the abstract; of narrowing their vision; of imbalance.

Magic is powerful; it is dangerous, as is anything which provokes change. One may be driven towards magic, be seduced by its glamours, or washed up against its shores through crisis, but it is most definitely *not* for all. No more than one would indiscriminately feed people powerful psychoactive drugs, or leave children to play with dangerous machinery. This is the seduction of technology, that its creators distance themselves from the uses to which their creations are put, and its glamours are seductive in the short-term, whereas the consequences are somewhat different. In the Sixties, we were fed the glamour of utopia through the harnessing of Nuclear Power. Thirty years later, the glamour has soured somewhat. It is the same with magic. What we imagine magic will enable us to become, and what we actually become after years of practice, are usually quite different.

The ability to perform advanced acts of magic requires years of effort; years of study, training, practice, analysis, and growing self-awareness. these years are valuable; the passage of time allows us to grow, to create our own codes of ethics and honours, forming the roots of our power, and the bedrock upon which we build our magical reality. As is often said, a powerful magician stands alone in the crowd, to some degree alien or inhuman.

Many yearn for this state, feeding the ego with feelings of superiority and the wish that others may see them as 'wise'. What is less often stated is that the adept magician, who feels his separateness all too keenly, is more likely to mourn the loss of innocence, if only secretly. One cannot shape the world without being reshaped in the process. Each gain of power requires its own sacrifice. The game of magical consequences never ends.

The emergence of Chaos Magic has given rise to a shift in the emphasis of modern magic. Sorcery, or magic which is directed towards an 'observable' result in the 'real' world, has, up until recently, thought to be "not quite the done thing", as opposed to the quest for 'Spiritual Perfection'. In the same way that scientists and mathematicians turned away from trying to get to grips with nature, which was, well, messy, and wouldn't always conform to neat formulae, and instead chose to examine events which were so small and abstract that it is difficult to see how they relate to everyday life. So much of magical practice relates to inner experience that it is all too easy for an individual to convince himself that he is a 'great magician' on the basis of inner experience alone, and not the ability to phenomenize that experience into action. Thus one tends to run into people who proclaim themselves to be magically potent, although it becomes clear that they are woefully impotent when it comes to matters of ordinary life.

STATEMENT OF INTENT

Consequently, if magic is to be effective, we must be able to Assess our performance, and moreover, relate the magical techniques that we use, to what emerges out of that use. Which is to say that if for example, you perform a ritual invocation of a particular entity for a specific purpose, you need to be able to be aware in what ways that ritual work resonates into your life. Chaos Magic addresses this issue by placing a rigorous emphasis on THE STATEMENT OF INTENT. All formalised acts of magic require a Statement of Intent, which is basically structured along the lines of "It is my will to [do something] for [a designated result]..." I will explore the practicalities of this in due course.

SELF-ASSESSMENT

In addition, Chaos Magic places an emphasis on Self-Assessment. Unfortunately, each individuals' capacity for self-delusion and blindness to problem areas does not somehow cease when a certain level of magical proficiency is attained. It is always easy to ignore or sweep aside that which does not fit into our dominant image of selfhood. In some magical or mystical systems, the responsibility of assessment is shifted onto a master or guru, someone who is supposed to have special insight into ones' character and know what is the 'right' thing for the student to do next. Within the Chaos approach, responsibility for action and movement rests ultimately with each individual. Certainly you may seek advice or different perspectives through any means open, from consulting with spirits, divinations, or asking your friends what they think, but the responsibility lies with you. The ability to examine your behavior, thoughts and feelings with a degree of dispassion and objectivity is a skill which, once you begin to use it, can be applied in any areas of your life.

MODELS AND METAPHORS

Despite the seeming complexity of occult theories—the hierarchies of inner planes, chakras, energy lines, archetypes, souls, akashic records, karmic debt recovery agencies and so forth, they tend to share a common tendency of rendering descriptions of the phenomenal world (where we spend most of our time) into very simple terms. Chaos Magic tends to reverse this kind of modeling, and tends to generate very simple models for describing abstract experience, while recognising the sometime need for using complex models for getting to grips with the phenomenal world. Peter Carroll, the foremost exponent of Chaos, points out that it is characterised by a "Cavalier" approach to metaphysics, based on the recognition that metaphysics are, after all, subject to belief. Many Occult belief systems consist of a hodge-podge of metaphysical speculations which are accepted as "truth", and which have additional bits 'bolted on' as those who create them try and cram anything and everything into the same model. Scientists once believed they could arrive at a grand theory of everything and anything. Occultists are attempting the same thing, although it tends to manifest as attempts to merge divergent systems such as the Tarot, Runes and I Ching together.

Chaos Magic however, is characterised by a willingness to use different models and learn from them. Thus Chaos Magicians use metaphors from Chaos Theory, Ecology, Biology, Psychology, Science Fiction, computer programming, management theory, and anything else which might prove interesting or potentially useful. The chapter in this book dealing with Chaos Servitors is a result of my studying the principles of programming a computer using the COBOL language. I never actually became adept at COBOL programming, but it gave me a useful perspective with which to examine the magical techniques I was using at the time. Using this particular model led me to wonder if some properties of the model were possible to transfer into magical action, and by experimentation, I found they were, although not quite in the way I had expected. Encountering new models and metaphors can sometimes fire us with enthusiasm for new explorations and creative leaps into the darkness of the unknown. But models, magical or otherwise, can become subtle traps. It seems all to easy for us to embrace a new model or reality-map, yet to suddenly find that we have bound ourselves within its limitations. But some models are particularly suited for specific tasks and situations. Rather than attempting to stretch one model so that it can account for everything and anything, the Chaos approach encourages one to use the model which is *most appropriate* to the situation. Some years ago, I was approached by an acquaintance who requested that I create a 'protective' talisman for her home. Now there are many different approaches to this kind of magic. It would have perhaps been easiest for me to create a 'shield' about her home, which could have been done without too much fuss or props. However, I wanted my acquaintance to 'feel' that something definite had been set up, so we opted for a ritual of angelic invocation using all the pomp and formality of the Qabalah, which left them in no doubt that mighty forces had been marshaled in order to protect the home from anything or anyone who might intrude with malign intent.

If our basic models of reality are changed, then suddenly, much of what we take for granted about the world can be called into question. It is a common tendency to behave *as if* our metaphors and maps are "True." If we choose to live according to the statement "Nothing is True," then we are bound to acknowledge the fragility of a metaphor as being no more than it is. Chaos has shifted the emphasis from seeking that which is 'magical' as that which lies beyond the known world, but recognising that the world itself is magical.

SELF AND OTHER

One of the most basic relationships is that of Self and Other; me and everything else; us and them. Even this relationship is informed by the dominant model of reality which is based on nineteenth century notions such as the absolute separation of mind from matter; the mechanical nature of the physical world and the distinction between subjectivity and objectivity. In this model, which is our consensual description of experienced reality, the mind makes sense of random, chance events which happen in the exterior, objective world. This is not so much an accurate description of the world, but a description that, on the grand scale, confirms and supports much of our self-conceits about humanities' relationship with the rest of the planet. Models tend to make the world a simpler place, shape experience to conform to our expectations, and also do a neat job of justifying our 'superior' position to everything else. A good example of such reductionist modeling is the creation of stereotypes. We all use stereotypes to varying degrees. They can be positive, acting as role models or ideal types, or negative stereotypes, which are responses to anxiety—loss of control. A simpler example yet is the tendency to describe our own behavior as a response to a given situation while attributing the behavior of others to their personality. A specific example within the magical context is that while you might well invoke deities, interpreting them as archetypes or subpersonalities, how far do you accept that those deities might have an existence, purpose and intentions that are separate and beyond your own? Thus, on various levels we ascribe meaning, intentionality and purposiveness to ourselves, and 'forget' about the 'Other'—be it other people or other species.

Where is this relevant to magic? Like many other basic patterns within our consensual reality, the consequences of the Self-Other distinction are rarely questioned. However, the Chaos Magic perspective demands that the magician be capable of looking 'behind the facade' of paramount reality for the underlying complexities and patterns. Chaos places an emphasis upon attention to detail, to being wary of the tendency to become uncritical of that which seems, on the surface, to be self-evident. On the more practical level of sorcery—the use of enchantments to actualise desire, it is all to easy to view a situation in terms of our own viewpoint being the most important, or that our perspective of an event is the only one that counts. The Ego Magic techniques of Chaos Magic allow you to shift perspectives and look at a situation from another person's viewpoint. The relativistic perspective of Chaos Magic emphasizes that situations and events are rarely as clear-cut as we would like them to be. There is also the question of how the 'Self' is regarded.

Although science has more or less driven out the religious concept of an immortal soul, it still tends to make a distinction between inner and outer experience by upholding the Mind-Body divide— *The Ghost in the Machine*. Magical theories which, like scientific theories, were codified and generalised in the Nineteenth century, tend to reinforce this division to various degrees. In contrast, Chaos supports the view that the Mind *arises* from the body. On the surface, this appears to be a reductionist argument, which is a criticism which has been leveled at Chaos Magic on more than one occasion. However, there is more to the concept than divesting ourselves of essentialist qualities. Many magicians use the term BodyMind to signify that Mind and Body should be considered a unified whole. If this can be accepted, then the whole subjective - objective distinction is called into question. Moreover, this viewpoint is supported by Chaos Science, which has not only highlighted the fact that the 'objective' world, which was once thought to be measurable, quantifiable and explainable following mathematical rules, has a high level of 'fuzziness' and indeter- minacy; but also that the 'subjective world' of the mind can be examined using analytical tools. Not only is there no 'Ghost' in the machine, but the idea of a physiological 'machine' moving through a passive environment has been shown up to be rather simplistic. Chaos philosophy is developing the idea of interdependent systems—ecologies—which have the inherent capacity for self-organisation. As a purely practical example, go out into woodlands or a similar 'natural' space. You are entering a dynamic ecosystem, whose elements include flora, fauna, local history, geographical and geological features, mythic associations, seasonal variations and weather. When you enter it, you become another element in a mesh of interrelated dynamics. Your experience of being within this place will depend upon your interaction with other elements, many of which you are likely to be unaware of (at least initially). Before you start to impose any 'magical' significance onto the place, observe it, be aware of your own relationship with it, and you might be surprised.

This illustrates another basic point about the Self-Other dynamic; that we can often be too eager when it comes to attributing meaning and interpretations onto a situation, and not allowing for other meanings to make themselves known. Rather than upholding 'differences' between Self and Other, Chaos Magic supports a celebration of diversity and difference. If "Nothing is True, Everything is Permitted", then there is no purpose or grand cosmic scheme to life beyond what we choose to impose or believe. To some this is cynicism. For the Chaos Magician, it is a breath of dizzying freedom.

ACHIEVABLE REALITY

Magic is a set of techniques and approaches which can be used to extend the limits of Achievable Reality. Our sense of Achievable Reality is the limitations which we believe bind us into a narrow range of actions and successes—what we believe to be possible for us at any one time. In this context, the purpose of magic is to simultaneously explore those boundaries and attempt to push them back—to widen the 'sphere' of possible action. Doubt and cynicism are dominant social attitudes in this last decade of the twentieth century. One of the first barriers that you will encounter is the doubt over whether magic can possibly 'work' in the first place. Like sex, magic needs to be experienced directly before it can be fully understood. A single act by which you demonstrate that MAGIC WORKS to yourself is worth a thousand books on so-called occult theory.

Much of what passes for magical theory is a hodge-podge of borrowed concepts, ranging from maps of the Inner Planes derived from Theosophy to popular psychology and 'alternative' physics. For the Chaos approach, the question of how much of it is "True" is irrelevant, since is the adoption of a belief which makes it viable, rather than its coherence. Most occult theories are treated in the same way as general scientific descriptions of the world. That is, they are presumed to be "true" independently of human experience and passed down from book to book without being questioned, and eventually pass into general acceptance, to the level that some people become quite upset if you don't appear to subscribe to them. This type of theory is known as *Theory-of-Action*. One of the problems that some people find when encountering Chaos Magic, is its tendency to discount orthodox magical theory, in favour of personal experience. However, there is another type of theory, *Theory-in-Use*, which is of greater use to the contemporary magician. Theory-in-Use relates to the guidelines and patterns that a magician learns, through personal experience and practice. Theories-in-Use cannot be taught, but arise out of the results of applying magic in your life. While books and other people can give you a knowledge of magical techniques, it is up to you as to how you apply them, and what theories and beliefs you weave around the results of your application. There are no 'correct' ways to perform magical acts, just the ones that work for you. Magic is about becoming more flexible, therefore you should not be surprised if you find yourself changing your ideas about magic from time to time.

MAGICAL POWER

It should also be understood that magic is not only concerned with pushing back the boundaries of Achievable Reality, but also understanding that some self-imposed limitations can be as much a source of power as a restriction. What is 'power' anyway? It is one of those words which gets thrown around a lot, and in magical writing tends to imply that a magician who is 'powerful' can summon dangerous demons, smite his enemies, and be attended upon by glamorous partners. There is also much talk of mysterious and subtle energies through which this power manifests. The word power has various definitions, among which are "the ability to act or produce an effect, the possession of control, influence or authority over others," and, as Bertrand

Russell put it, "the ability to achieve intended effect." This latter definition is closest to understanding 'magical power.'

A confusion has arisen in recent years over the relationship between power and the core tenet of Chaos Magic, that "nothing is true, and everything is permitted." Some critics have chosen to interpret this as meaning that the whole point of Chaos Magic is to throw away all restrictions and find power in absolute freedom. This is both a misunderstanding of the Chaos approach, and a misunderstanding of the nature of power. Absolute power, without restraints, is a fiction in the modern world. Anywhere that you choose to look for an example of someone who is 'powerful,' look closer and you will find that power is severely constrained. Take for example the American hostage crisis in Iran. Theoretically, the then president, Jimmy Carter, had the power to reduce Iran to smoking rubble within minutes. Although Carter had the military power to do this, it could not actually be done. In the light of this, a more appropriate definition of magical power might be that it is the ability to achieve intended effect within the constraints of a given situation. A common misunderstanding of magical power is that it somehow allows the magician to exercise control *over* aspects of reality, and a distinction has arisen between "power-over" (bad) and "power-from-within" (good). The term "power-over" is used to describe the wielding of power against another, by physical, legal, or financial means. Whereas "power-from-within" is the very personal sense of 'being able' which arises out of acts of creativity or magic. This distinction has its value, in that it enables us to understand that magical power is something that we feel within, rather than an external agency. Next, there comes the issue of so-called *magical* powers such as telepathy, levitation, influencing people (and events) at a distance, sensing auras, precognition or for that matter, bending spoons. In Tantra, such abilities are known as *Siddhis,* a word which is generally translated as "achievements." Something which is an achievement is the result of practice, discipline and patience. If you ever do meet a magician who can seemingly do marvelous things at the drop of hat, it is a fairly safe bet he has been practicing for a very long time.

Magic is the quest for power—the ability to achieve intended effect. You become 'powerful' in this sense, when you have demonstrated to yourself (and others, if you are working in a group or in touch with other magicians) that you can make manifest your intention, to the point where you are confident and relaxed—that magic is not so much something that you 'do', but an expression of your being. The understanding of the limits and constraints which channel your power, is the difference between the effective magician and the megalomaniac. Chaos Magic is not about discarding all rules and restraints, but the process of discovering the most effective guidelines and disciplines which enable you to effect change in the world.

MAGICAL REALITY: THE TWILIGHT ZONE

Magic is a two-way process; you use it to change yourself and in return, it changes you. Letting yourself enter a magical reality is not about creating an enclave of magic beyond your everyday life, but of allowing magic *in*—allowing for the intrusion of the weird, the irrational, the things you can't explain, yet are undeniably real. You may well learn the summoning of spirits using ritual magic, but what happens when the spirits summon you? Encounters with strange lights, half-glimpsed figures, rushing presences and flickering lights; these are very much associated with the wilderness—they come with the territory. But what do you do when magic comes a'calling around into your house?

There is no script or teaching on this subject. You learn by live experience and listening to your fellows. This is truly the intrusion of the Twilight Zone—the fuzzy borderlines that we draw between common, everyday experience, and the more-than-real. What is it about these experiences that is important? Firstly, that they are real in a way that overcomes all rationalisations to the contrary. Whenever I am in the presence of strangeness, I shiver and tears prick up at the corners of my eyes. I know and value this response, as it allows me to sort out the difference between 'real' strangeness and an over-active imagination. Secondly, they are often shared by others. A magician deals with gods, demons, spirits, elementals and what have you. It is easy, therefore, to slip into a mental attitude of thinking that all these diverse entities are only at your beck and call, and have no existence or will beyond yours. This attitude tends to fragment when a spirit turns up unannounced, especially if other people meet it too. A common feature of such experiences is that we tend to behave 'normally' within them. It is only afterwards that we realise and say "what the Fu...". A few years ago, a visiting friend came back from the bathroom and told me that there was a "thing" on the landing. Intrigued, I went out to have a look at this "thing" and found a moving shadow, roughly six feet high and man-shaped, in the half-light of the stairwell. We proceeded to question this entity and found it to be evasive, although promising that it would "give you power". Unsatisfied with its answers, we told it to leave us alone. It was only afterwards that the uncanniness of the whole experience hit us. It was particularly amusing that although we accepted the presence of the unknown entity unreservedly, we had been highly skeptical of the answers it had given us to our questions. and dismissed it when it would not give us the quality of information that we required.

This sort of behavior appears to be common, at least from the people I have talked to about such intrusions of the uncanny. We do what seems to be appropriate at the time, and only afterwards does the shock of the bizarre hit us. And it may be a shock indeed. When people ask me "is magic dangerous?" I remember an experience of a friend some years ago. She was just getting to grips with goddess-consciousness, having come through feminist politicization, but still dealing with Catholic guilt. I had lent her boyfriend a copy of Aleister Crowley's Hymn to Pan. She found it one night, and read it. She said it stirred mixed feelings of excitement and revulsion as emotional sparks and beliefs warred within her. Filled with a curious tension and apprehension, she reached up to a bookshelf and knocked down her boyfriend's Tarot pack. 'The Devil' landed face up, down at her feet. At that moment, she said, her entire world cracked apart. Now I could say that the experience was a manifestation of Chaos, or a synchronicity—but such terms are almost irrelevant. What matters is that it happened, and nothing was the same again. This is magic indeed. I don't think it is possible to go out searching for such encounters—they come to us. Hence the term 'Twilight Zone'—the UFOnauts never appear to the believer, but to the 'ordinary person' next door. But there do seem to be some shades of awareness and perception that help, while others hinder. Physical exhaustion which leaves you alert seems to be beneficial, for instance. Mental exhaustion, on the other hand, appears to dull your sensitivity to intrusions from the outside. The appropriate mental attitude I would say is very much on the level of "what happens, happens." This is echoed by Austin Osman Spare's doctrine of "Does not matter—Need not be"— again, a form of relaxation in the present environment. You need to have a level-headed 'matter-of-fact' approach to this kind of experience. Explanations don't matter, experience does. Someone asks "Do you believe in Ghosts?" No. Which is not to say that I've never seen things which could be explained as ghosts. Not at all. It's just that I haven't taken up the common beliefs and explanations of ghosts. Again, this is a core message of Chaos Magic. You don't have to believe in Past Lives, Chakras, Reincarnation Hidden Adepts and the Astral Plane to work effective magic. If you want to believe in any/all of this and more, then it's your choice. Similarly, you don't have to believe in something to suddenly have it walk up to you and ask for a light. I used to believe that magic was merely psychology dressed up. That is, until one night I awoke to find something heavy and misty sitting upon my chest. Yes, okay, I admit it—I was scared shitless! I lay there for what felt like an eternity until I mentally visualised a pentagram and projected it forth, and the 'thing' promptly faded away. I was in shock for days. Now I've heard lots of different explanations from other people, but what is important for me is that it showed me, more convincingly than any argument or book, that magic is something real.

CHAPTER THREE

BECOMING A MAGICIAN

Becoming a magician takes time, and practice, and experience. It is not just a matter of reading a few books, trying out a few exercises, rituals, and so forth, and then declaring yourself to be a magician. Sadly, it is all too easy for us to convince ourselves about our suitability for something. When Aleister Crowley wrote that "magic is for ALL," few seem to have considered that he was possibly overstating the case. A thorough examination of Crowley's life, particularly the number of his associates who tried to be magicians, yet failed; who's lives ended in madness or misery—clearly indicates that magic is NOT for everyone. A magician is a person who recognises that the world he moves through is an extremely complex place; that all that seems apparent and clear-cut, in actuality, hides a seething complexity, the full depths of which he may never grasp. Such a person, by necessity, is continually on guard against that which might limit his ability to adapt and survive in this world. A magician is constantly aware of his inner structures, and that which is around him. He constantly strives to extend his possibilities for action, patient, yet aware of the necessity sometimes, of going *too far* in all directions. Magic, in some senses, is the science of extremes. Many people are attracted to the occult as an attempt to escape from the responsibility of being human. Many seem to want to gain magical powers immediately, without sacrifice or responsibility to that power. But the kind of abilities that a magician may develop cannot be bought over the counter like a Saturday-night special. Magical 'powers' are literally the result of one's discipline; they are the result of practice, study, and the application of theories and techniques in one's own life. Moreover, this process is one that changes you. With power, comes the understanding of responsibility. It is my responsibility as a writer to say that no one ever became a magician from reading books. Sure, you can learn from other people, but you don't become a magician until you begin to twist something that you have read or learned, and apply it successfully within your own life. Anyone can convince themselves that they are a magician in the safety of their own heads; it helps sometimes to have a few followers or friends who agree—but the test here, is to go somewhere else and be a magician there. One of the most significant 'powers' a magician develops is a certain poise—a degree of self-assured assurance of manner. A good magician maintains this poise, no matter where he is, or who he has about him. This is a power that other magicians can recognise and respect, as it says much more about a person than what he says about himself.

In magical circles, there is sometimes a degree of confusion over the distinction between 'basic' and 'advanced' magic. The former is associated with 'beginners', while the latter is associated with adepts or magi. Some people seem to have the opinion that 'basic' techniques of magic should only be practiced for a set period, and then discarded in favour of something more arcane. In the Chaos approach, the term 'basic' applies to any technique or practice which is simple, effective, and which, once understood, can be applied throughout your life, no matter how far advanced a magician you may become.

PREPARING FOR MAGICAL PRACTICE

To learn any magical techniques and skills requires Practice, just as does learning to read, write, or drive a car. Practice is difficult, especially nowadays, when we are increasingly becoming used to the idea of 'instant' courses, remedies, and therapies.

One weekend workshop does not make you a 'magician', any more than one weekend of driving a car would make you a proficient motorist. To become skilled requires time, effort, and self-discipline. When learning magical techniques, we are often going through a process of extending our everyday range of abilities, often in ways that may not have occurred to us previously. This requires a level of determination that will, at times, seem onerous, or 'more effort than it's worth', and the benefits may only seem obvious in the long-term.

There are two elements that are worth considering when it comes to Practice. The first is that we are learning new skills that will form a sound basis for further work. There is little point attempting to work entirely on the 'astral plane' if you cannot sit still for five minutes or hold an image in your mind's eye without wandering off onto another track. Practice requires discipline, and the growth of self-discipline is in itself a powerful magical ally. If nothing else, by assiduously doing something which you have promised to yourself that you will do—you are increasing your confidence in your ability to do things—and confidence is a key to successful magic.

The second element to consider is that in setting yourself a goal of regular practice, you are pitting yourself against what is probably your most deadly magical adversary—your own inertia. If you have a conversation with yourself that you are "lazy, unable to concentrate, and can never finish tasks off", then the only way to break out of that self-imposed limitation is to set yourself a regular practice and do it! You may well be surprised at your own ingenuity in trying to wriggle out from doing the practice: that it'd be much better to have a lie in than get up and meditate, that you'll do it twice tomorrow for missing out today, that you don't possibly have the 'spare' time.

At times the limitations we impose upon ourselves seem to have a life of their own. They resist being changed by fighting against the changes that we are trying to make in our lives. It may be that, if we do not find a new task difficult and imposing on everyday life, we are not taking it seriously enough. Only when we take up something that threatens our established patterns do our limitations seek to preserve themselves, so the fact that you might be coming up with attractive excuses to keep you from practice can be taken as a good sign. But the only way you will change the pattern is to keep trying until you change it. This often requires determination, tenaciousness, and sheer bloody-mindedness—all in themselves, qualities that are useful for the budding magician.

THE MAGICAL DIARY

The Magical Diary is an ally to practice, a work record, and confessor. Astronomers often say that "if it wasn't written down, it didn't happen," and this is a good axiom for magicians to take up. Keeping a magical diary is a good habit to get into, enabling you record all of your attempts at different exercises and techniques, any ideas and insights that arise from them, and anything else that you find significant. Years later, you might look back at your early attempts and squirm uncomfortably, but equally, you will find that having a record of work in this way is very useful, since magical ideas and insights often loop back into earlier experiments. It is not unknown for magicians to start developing an idea, put it aside, and come back to it years later with a fresh understanding and insight into what it was about. The same thing tends to happen with books. You might read a book and have no idea what the author is really saying—then come back to it later, and find that, in the light of your accumulated experience, it makes much more sense. It is also worth bearing in mind that, as most magicians bring their own insights and personal views into developing their own approaches and specialties in magic, a diary is a record of your doings that one day, historians might find a valuable document!

You should choose a method of keeping a diary which is most convenient to you—such as in a bound, blank-page book, a ring-binder folder, or even on a computer disk. The sort of information that should be included in diary write-ups includes:

1. What was done
2. Duration
3. Where it was done
4. Any pertinent weather, Moon phase, Astrological conjunctions (if you feel these are significant to you)
5. How you felt it went
6. Any ideas arising from it
7. Any other comments

Some magical teachers and groups insist that students be prepared to present their diaries for scrutiny. It can be a useful spur to keep your diary 'as though' someone was going to look at it at some stage.

TIME

Regular practice takes time, which is a commodity that not all of us have in the same degree. For example, many practical magic workbooks recommend that you assiduously do a particular practice at the same hour, each day. This is fine is your lifestyle allows you to rigorously plan your day, but for others, it is impossible. In setting up your own schedules for practice, it is essential that you be realistic about the amount of 'free time' that you can allot to practice. If you absolutely cannot do a daily practice, then give yourself a schedule that you know you have a better chance of keeping to. It is only useful to set practice schedules if you know that you can realistically find the free space to stick to them. If you set an unrealistic practice schedule then it is likely you will not be able to keep to it—which will not improve your confidence. I have found that on average, it is better to practice an exercise for a short time frequently, than for a long period infrequently—so that five minutes of meditation on a daily basis is more beneficial than half an hour every three weeks. Likewise, it is easier to begin some exercises by attempting them for a few minutes, and then to slowly increase the duration, than to try and strain yourself. There's no point in trying to run before you can walk, especially when it comes to magic, where it is very easy to fall flat on your face.

TAKING A BREAK

One point that must be taken into account is that it is very easy to get into a situation where you find that you have 'overloaded' yourself with magical work to do. This is not good practice, as it is increasing the possibility that you will get bogged in inertia. If you find that this is the case, then take a 'holiday' from active magical work. This is particularly useful if you find yourself reading too many magical books, without giving yourself time to assimilate their contents. Taking a break from active magical work can be a magical act in its own right. Set a period during which you don't read any magical texts, or do any active practice, other than perhaps, a simple daily meditation. Paradoxically, you may find this difficult to do, particularly if you have placed a good deal of importance on 'becoming' a magician. By giving yourself a short breathing-space, you will find that you can approach practice with a renewed freshness.

STAGES OF LEARNING

When learning a new skill, there are three stages that we go through, which it is well to be aware of. When we initially begin some new practice, there is (hopefully) a high level of enthusiasm. The results of the practice are good, and we can feel the benefits of what we are doing. So far so good. At some stage though, we pass into the 'dry' phase of acquiring the skill. At this point, it becomes BORING. This is the time when all the excuses for not doing something, all the little get-out clauses that we resort to are at their most powerful. It is the 'hump' that students on long degree courses experience, and the phase when it seems easier to give up rather than push on. Indeed, many people do quit magical development at this stage, as they suddenly find that the benefits they have experienced earlier, suddenly dry up and vanish. Our advice is to grit your teeth and hang on in there—it won't last forever (though at times, it might seem like it). If you can get over the 'hump', then you may well be surprised to find that gradually, you feel different about what you're doing—that you can see the benefit of something that, for a time, you felt was pointless and boring and, even, that you're quite enjoying it. A lot of our early learning is like this, though we tend to forget how teachers pushed us to read, write and add up—the process moves from being a new, enjoyable 'game', to being a boring imposition, to being something that we one day realise that we can do 'without effort'. A great deal of magical skills and abilities, from meditation to clairvoyance, are learned in this way.

SELF-ASSESSMENT

This is the ability to make judgements about your own progression. As magic can be at times, a nebulous subject with vague terms of reference, self-assessment can be difficult. A great part of some magical systems is the development of a symbolic frame of reference in which the student can place herself in terms of where she is, where she was, and where she is going. As you will see in the following section on 'Magical Dangers', it is all too easy for magicians to develop an inflated sense of their own enlightenment, but equally, it is similarly easy to deny according yourself with making any progress at all. The magical diary is a great help here. You may not think that you've progressed in a given length of time, but providing you've been keeping a record of your practice, then you should be able to see some differences between when you began the practice, and where you are now. Being able to assess yourself is an important, yet sometimes underrated aspect of magical development. Some students turn to teachers or 'gurus' to tell them 'where they are', which can bring its own problems, especially if one comes to expect the guru to take total responsibility for everything, and some so-called teachers are only too willing to do this. When it comes down to it, the one who knows you best, of course, is yourself. Thus you must grit your teeth and be prepared to acknowledge (in your diary) your weak areas and the conversations which you have with yourself to convince yourself that you "can't do..." It can be useful to divide a page into two columns and list your perceived strengths and weaknesses; what you would like to change, and how you perceive magic as being able to help you change. "Know Thyself" was the admonition to the initiate in the Greek Eulesian Mysteries, and it remains a core axiom for magicians to this present day.

IS MAGIC DANGEROUS?

Though it is rarely admitted, there are certain pitfalls that magicians are prone to, and even the most advanced of us can end up in them. Some of the pitfalls associated with the practice of magic are:

Isolation

Isolation precedes madness—yet most 'how to' books on magic are written for the solo practitioner. Although magicians tend to be individualists, it is well to remember that we are social beings too, and we rarely grow in isolation to others—hence a major reason for the existence of magical orders, groups, and courses. Although not everyone likes working in a group, it is nonetheless useful to have someone with whom you can discuss your ideas, progress, problems and feelings with. Even if people do not share your interests, a sympathetic ear is often helpful. Magic is not about retreating from the world, but a way of becoming more effective within it. If you can't communicate what's going on inside you to another person, and likewise, are unable to 'hear' other people's opinions, then it is very easy to end up in some of the other pitfalls.

Magus-itis

Some books on magic tend to give the impression that a Magus is someone who can do 'anything', from crossing the abyss overnight to balancing his checkbook. Magus-itis covers the syndrome for people who, despite what their peers think of them, feel themselves to have reached some exalted state, which is usually synonymous with behaving like a complete arsehole. It is very easy for magicians to convince themselves that they are the best thing since 'sliced bread' and hence 'above' everyone else, given automatic respect, and are obviously more 'important'. Sadly, the sufferer of Magus-itis tends to be seen by others as a figure of scorn, pity, fun, or someone to avoid at all costs. Their inflated sense of their own importance is rarely shared by anyone else, and their antics often put other people 'off' the idea of becoming a magician. Sufferers often display an intense desire to be a Guru or Teacher, presumably so that they can acquire a captive audience who will reinforce their sense of being 'right' in the face of all evidence to the contrary. As they find it difficult to accept that anyone could possibly be at their level of 'illumination', they lack the ability to develop the empathy, communication and social skills that makes for an effective teacher. In short, if you think that you are wonderful, but no one else seems to agree, then it's time to have a very close look at yourself.

Obsession

Obsession is not a danger that is exclusive to magic. You can become obsessed about anything, from sex to train-spotting, but the common factor present in all obsessions is that you can't talk about anything else. Being obsessed with magic is a popular trip; I've done it myself—constantly going on about magic to all and sundry, regardless of whether or not they're really interested and, if the conversation turns to something beyond magic, suddenly feeling uncomfortable.

Then there's the 'sinister' behavior that sometimes manifests, cultivating a glamour of being an 'outsider', and staring into people's eyes. This is often a cover for a lack of social skills, and a gnawing sense of inferiority.

Cosmic Tragedy

Those who enter the world of magic often feel a sense of tremendous urgency to put the world to rights, become 'illuminated' and do all manner of idealistic things in a tremendous hurry. Suddenly, everything that happens, takes on a 'magical' significance. So too, one's fears, worries and problems take on a cosmic dimension to the level where you're not merely 'going through a bad patch', but are having a cosmic initiation that no one else can possibly understand, and is vital to the future of the human race.

Paranoia

It's amazing how quickly we can, either alone or in a group, generate an atmosphere of magical paranoia, which tends to create a situation where something 'odd' is likely to happen—which of course is then going to be seen as 'evidence' for an attack being under way. And then what happens? That's right, you start looking for 'enemies'. Ah, but, you might say, magical attack does happen. Well yes it does, but I would argue that nine times out of ten one only has to look in a mirror to see the source of the 'bad vibes'. Over the last fifteen years or so, I've only detected three magical attacks (which is surprising, given the talent I seem to have for upsetting people) of which, each has been corroborated by other people and which fortunately, I've been able to do something about at the time. But I've met any amount of 'occultists' who were convinced that they were under attack by Satanists, Black Lodges, Chaos Magicians, etc. etc.

Gnostic Burn-Out

Gnostic Burn-out occurs when you have been 'overdoing it' magically. Often this is a case of too many rituals in a very short space of time, or a result of not thoroughly grounding yourself after a particularly heavy session. Some people are of the opinion that if you're a 'good' magician, then this shouldn't happen. Personally, I am of the opinion that if you're a 'good' magician, then you have to expect this sort of occurrence as your practice propels you into weird states of consciousness, strange bodily sensations, and downright weirdness. My own response to episodes of Gnostic Burnout is to go off and have a good lie down, and support from other people helps, too.

Where possible, Chaos Magic uses simple explanations for magical techniques, relating them very much to aspects of everyday experience. Belief in concepts such as chakras, the astral plane, karma, reincarnation, auras, magical energies, cosmic powers and so forth is optional and a matter of personal taste. But you don't have to believe in any of this to work effective magic. Nor is magic something which stands apart from the rest of your life. Magic is not so much something which you do occasionally behind closed doors or in the space behind your closed eyes, but a way of living your life—a way of approaching the world you move through and everything in it.

Some Magical Workbooks tend to give the impression that you become a magician by experimenting with practical exercises, taking on particular beliefs, and learning a specialist vocabulary with which you can talk to other magicians. For the moment, I want to pose the question, "what makes a good magician?" As I have intimated, being a magician is something more than merely dressing up in a black robe, attempting to cast spells, invoke gods and use strange terminology that only other "initiates" understand. Being a "good" magician, at least from the relativistic perspective of Chaos Magic, is being effective and adaptive in as many areas of one's life as possible. To expand on this definition further I will examine five key qualities associated with effective magicians.

THE QUALITIES OF C.H.A.O.S

This acronym represents Confidence, Honour, Attentiveness, Organisation and Sensitivity. These qualities are of use in not only specifically 'magical' situations, but in life generally, and so are of 'global' application.

Confidence

Confidence is usually a trait associated with magicians. It is generally accepted that a good magician is 'confident'—but what actually does this mean? Confidence is usually described as a quality that people possess to varying degrees. We "gain" or "lack" confidence, yet it is also perceived that being "over-confident" is a negative trait, so that overall, confidence seems to be something which is finely balanced. For the present discussion, I will define confidence as a skill: *the skill of being relaxed in the immediate present.* I shall explain what I mean by that as follows... A person who lacks confidence in general, tends not to attempt something which lies outside his rehearsed repertoire of behaviors—he fears the possible consequences of moving into an unknown area—be they imagined, or predicated from past experience. Similarly, a person who is over-confident may attempt something and fail, as he is limited by 'gazing' into a future where he has already succeeded, and so his attentiveness to the immediate present is blunted. If one is relaxed within the immediate present, then one is neither projecting/anticipating future scenarios, nor is one limited by the boundaries created by previous experience and past conditioning. Here, the ability to relax refers to being aware—attentive, of the immediate present, without rigidly patterning that present as it unfolds.

Confidence is also situation-dependent. We tend to say that confidence is required through practice at something. One may practice a ritual until one may perform it totally seamlessly, but that does not automatically imply that one will be totally confident performing it while three hundred people are watching. People tend to be confident in areas which are familiar, and not so confident when they enter new territory. This is particularly true of magic, which almost by definition necessitates a movement into uncharted territory. I have often observed how people who are very much 'experts' in their chosen fields can become spectacularly nervous and unsure of themselves when placed in a "magical" situation. If we lack confidence in a situation, we are not relaxed, and so tend to make mistakes. There is a very powerful conditioning-directive which says that "mistakes are bad." Being seen to make mistakes is bad for one's ego, and worse in terms of social status. If we do something, we have to be seen to be "good" at it, if not "expert". Anything else is anathema to the self-image.

This is a potentially dangerous trap to fall into. Many a muddled magical theorem has managed to maintain itself against attempts at analysis or destruction, precisely because such a meme, when delivered by figure who has authority status, is extremely difficult to challenge. Gurus and belief-systems form a safety-net for those who, while feeling a need to step beyond the boundaries of their consensus reality, yet feel massively afraid at the same time. Consider also, the experience of 'viability of magic' as an issue of confidence. One occasionally hears people making remarks to the effect that they are confident about magic's viability when it is 'working' for them, but that when life 'goes wrong', then explanations such as karma, tides, psychic attack, etc. are trotted out. One of the core components of confidence is a recognition that the world is chaotic, rather than linear. We tend to model events in a linear fashion, and then behave as though everything will always conform to our expectations. Of course, it is often difficult to remain relaxed as a crisis bursts over us, as emotions, memories, fantasy projections, internal dialogues and learned response patterns struggle for supremacy. This recognition of chaotic flow can be discerned in the ways in which we "frame" new experiences—particularly, new learning. New situations tend to generate performance anxiety, due to their unfamiliarity. Stepping into a situation where there are many unknown possibilities and contingencies, we find it difficult to transfer confidence; that is, to stay relaxed, and to still the little doubts and fears. If one can work within the proposition that such new situations are not 'difficult', but "novel", then any physical sensation can be reframed as excitement. When interest and curiosity are engaged towards a novel situation, we tend to pay more attention to what is going on in the environment, rather than the demons of the ego. In other words, there is a common tendency to, when faced with a new or unfamiliar situation, to label it as difficult and frightening, and then retreat from it. This raises anxiety and hence difficulty becomes a self-fulfilling prophecy. If, on the other hand, the unfamiliar can be approached as novelty, then awareness is engaged towards the situation.

Confidence is also transferable. If one is skilled in confidence, then one can project it, so that others become confident. Numerous examples of such occurrences can be discerned in all areas of human activity. This phenomenon plays an important role in group magical events.

As discussed above, confidence is a skill which centres around relaxation. Relaxation promotes attentiveness to subtle conditions in the environment. As is well-known, relaxation also short-circuits "Lust of Result." which, in terms of confidence, is equivalent to the tendency to generate fantasy outcomes. But Lust of Result can be more than simply worrying about the outcome of a sigil. Lust of Result can cover individuals' concerns over group performance, anxiety over the unfamiliar, forgetting one's lines, etc. A magician skilled in confidence projection can act as an 'anchor' for others present, so that they may relax into the present, and interpret bodily arousal as excitement, rather than anxiety. Understanding the dynamics, and becoming skilled at being confident is a basic requirement for effective magic.

Having stressed the relationship between confidence and relaxation, it should be remembered that Preparation is also necessary for confidence. Not only must one be attentive of subtle changes and chaotic fluctuations, but one also has to *Be Prepared.* This means knowing your material, and having a range of strategies open to you. One approach to the reframing of anxiety-based projections is to use them to mentally rehearse scenarios. Research from the American Department of Defense indicates that people who mentally rehearse their range of responses to difficult situations calmly, tend to be more relaxed when placed in a 'live' situation.

For a magician then, being confident is the ability to relax when faced with unfamiliar or anxiety-creating situations. It is also related to the ability to experience the unfamiliar as novel or exciting. Confidence is also a key to successful magic, and I will discuss techniques that demonstrate this shortly. If someone is (apparently) confident performing magical rituals alone, yet nervous and ill-at-ease in any other situation, then they have missed the point of Chaos Magic.

A byproduct of confidence is Neophilia—the tendency to be open to new ideas and concepts. Generally, people who are relaxed and confident do not feel that they have to defend themselves or their chosen beliefs/ideologies. Thus good magicians tend to be open-minded and relaxed—fanaticism and the need to proselytise tend to be the behaviors of those who lack self-confidence unless surrounded by the safe and familiar.

Honour

Most quasi-religious or transcendentalist magical systems are characterised by an ethical code which is external to individuals, laid down in some 'holy book', and almost always broken. Far better, then, to develop one's own personal rules. It may seem an odd statement for a Chaos Magician to make, but I believe that having a personal honour code enhances one's ability as a magician. For example, over the years I have developed my own personal 'rules' about magical acts directed at other people, and will not deviate from them unless a situation fulfills fairly specific criteria. Furthermore, being seen to be 'honorable' in specific ways impresses other people, building one's credibility as an effective magician, and as someone who can be relied upon. A sense of honour determines ones actions, and it is usually by actions, rather than words or postures, that one is judged by others. If you like, the points of honour that you decide to live by are the foundations of your personal psychocosm. It is also worth remembering that words have power. If you believe that your words can unleash power and bind entities to your will, then it follows that your own words can bind you too.

Points of Honour

Your Word is Your Bond. Avoid placing yourself in a situation where your integrity can be questioned. Be aware that other people, particularly other magicians, are continually looking at your reputation. It can take years to establish yourself as an magician; but you can blow your reputation away in a single evening.

If I say so, I will try
If I say I shall, I will do
If I say "I promise", I am bound

If you say you will do something, then you MUST do it. If you are dependable, people will have confidence in you. The more confidence they have in you, the more powerful a magician you will become. Equally, if you cannot realistically do some-thing, then it is a mark of quality to say that you cannot do it. This point is particularly pertinent if you choose to perform magic on behalf of other people.

Resolve Problems. If problems occur, they should be dealt with as soon as possible. The longer a problem is left, the less likely it is that it will be resolved. If a problem relating to another person cannot be resolved, then contact them as soon as possible anyway. Prompt dealing with problems is generally appreciated.

Admit Errors. It is better to admit a mistake, freely, and without reservation, than to attempt to cover it up. This also builds credibility, providing, of course, you do something about the problem.

These points are mostly related to how you deal with other people. From the perspective of Chaos Magic, the mark of an effective magician is the ability to deal effectively with other people, in a wide range of life situations. If you strive to uphold these points of honour (and others) towards other people, then you will be more likely to apply them to yourself.

Attentiveness

Situations are more complex and subtle than most people are willing to recognise. It pays to be attentive to what is happening around you. Beware of being over-confident or too tense. Beware of anything that dulls your attentiveness to others. The practice of Deconditioning (which I shall discuss in due course) is important in this respect. You must be able to distinguish between the world as it is, and how you would like it to be. One example which demonstrates this necessity is Conversational Feedback.

If you are talking to someone else with a specific purpose in mind, such as convincing them of the need to buy a product, then it should be fairly obvious that you need to pay attention to the way in which they respond to what you are saying. Such feedback can be verbal (words, tone of voice) and non-verbal (facial response, body posture, etc.) and, in order to be effective, you will need to be able to correctly interpret the other's reaction and change your tactics accordingly. Often though, people do not pay attention to feedback, as their attention has been diverted. This may be due to lack of, or over-confidence in the situation. In other words, they have already decided the outcome (either as success or failure) and are unwilling to let anything that the other person says alter their conclusion. Another reason may be that the speaker has invested so much self-importance in what he is saying, that the listener's response is not important.

It may help, in this regard, to discuss the quality of Intuition as a refined form of attentiveness. Intuition is often referred to in terms of being a mysterious "sixth" sense which is somehow related to psychic powers and the like. This reflects how we model the cognitive patterns which we use to make conclusions, rather than anything mysterious or paranormal. Partially, the ability we call intuition is the capacity to arrive at decisions without moving through the process of conscious logical deduction. Another key part of this ability is our skill at being able to recognise very small sensory cues and gain an overall impression (a gestalt) again, without using linear cognition. What is also of interest is that "intuitional" responses often seem to appear without being prompted—when we are relaxed, or not thinking about the subject of the thought. Intuition is also contextual. When I worked as a therapist in a busy psychiatric department, I found that I was beginning to make 'snap' diagnoses of clients, without having had access to their case notes and that in at least eight out of ten cases, I proved to be right. A few years later, I began to lead seminars in magical training, and I found that in time, I could make fairly accurate distinctions between people who had, during an exercise, entered a fairly deep level of trance, and those who were 'faking' it. In each case, I knew what signs to look for, and was processing, very rapidly, a wide variety of feedback cues without being aware of anything but the cognitive outcome.

Like confidence, attention can be considered to be a skill. One level of the skill is training yourself to be very aware of your environment at any time, while at the same time remaining detached, empty of preconceptions and expectations, and above all, relaxed. Another level of the skill is learning to accept whatever impressions arise in your mind without dismissing them, or, for that matter, latching onto them to the extent that later impressions are excluded. To be effective, a magician needs to be attentive not only to his external surroundings, but to his own emotions, motivational complexes, desires, habits and internal dialogues.

Organisation

A contemporary definition of magic is that it is "an organisation of the imagination." To be effective in the world, organisation is required, whatever one is doing. In the course of writing this book, I have had to lay down a sequence of themes which I wanted to develop through the narrative. Similarly, to perform a magical ritual, I have to prepare a framework of organised coherence. As noted earlier, there is a great tendency to view approaches to magic as systems. There are the variants of Qabalah, Wicca, Shamanism, Satanism, etc. Many of these systems have models of symbolically ordering and representing the universe. Some are highly abstract, such as western Qabalah, while others have varying degrees of interpenetration with everyday experience. Generally, we use such models to structure, interpret, and evaluate magical experiences. Some champions of these approaches have criticized Chaos Magic as they feel that the term Chaos implies disorder and that Advocates of Chaos Magic are proposing a disorganised approach to magic. This is largely due to a misperception of the Chaos approach, which tends to view the use of magical systems as a matter for personal preference. As I have already shown, the term Chaos need not refer to disorder, and similarly, being organised need not mean that you have assigned everything to a rigid place and cannot deviate from it, but that you have prepared yourself in readiness for action.

Is organisation a skill? Obviously so, for it improves with practice, and your effectiveness in organising yourself will depend on your skill at being relaxed and attentive. If you make organisation an important point in your honour code, then other people will view you as effective and competent, which will tend to increase your effectiveness even further. Obviously, there is a feedback loop in operation here. If you have organised yourself in preparation for a task, then you will find it easier to relax when performing the task, and consequently, the more confident you can be concerning its outcome. Your ability to structure your thoughts, and identify key areas in a situation which require particular attention is also a key to practical sorcery.

Strive for Excellence. In a way, this is the axis of the whole issue of being a magician. Being a magician is not a state of being, but a dynamic engagement. There is no zero state of having "made it"—there is only more to do. Becoming an Adept, in many ways, is tantamount to becoming very good at doing lots of things. The more you practice magic, the more you will discover about yourself, other people, and the world in general. Do what you will to do, to the best of your ability.

Erudition. If you would aspire to teach, to lead, or to inspire, then you need to have not only knowledge of, but confidence in, your chosen field. A worthy comment from Robert Anton Wilson in this respect is that "specialisation is for insects." Powerful magicians have a wide-ranging interest that crosses into many different fields, but they are bound by none of them. Similarly, it is not enough to have access to specialised knowledge. Great care must be taken as to how that knowledge is expressed.

Sensitivity

Being sensitive does not mean that you are fragile; that as a result of an adverse comment, you shrink away and spend the next six weeks hiding from everyone else. No, here I am referring to a wide range of skills which include discrimination, prudence, tact, care, and empathy. To be sensitive requires that you have an awareness of the needs and emotions of other people. Indeed, sensitivity can extend into the level of perception which we tend to associate with psychic powers and intuited thoughts which turn out to be correct. Again, sensitivity is a skill which can be learned. At its simplest level, it is the art of listening to what others are saying. Much of what I have written about Attention is pertinent here, but Sensitivity requires that you not only be aware of subtle nuances in a situation, but that you can react appropriately—with intelligence, prudence and tact. The skill of sensitivity is a further illustration of the Self-Other distinction discussed in the previous chapter. We are often too 'caught up' in our own self-images to really pay attention to other people, or even to take account of other people's feelings in a situation. If for example, I am too concerned with what I think other people are thinking about me, then I am not going to be sensitive to their actual reactions. Moreover, it is unlikely that I will be able to respond effectively if I am too concerned with myself. Again, sensitivity requires relaxation. Sensitivity also requires that we are aware of complexities, especially given the common tendency to reduce any situation so that it conforms with our expectations. For example it is all too easy to believe that people who share common interests with us will be similar in other ways. This is obviously not the case, if we stop and think about it, but in a 'live' situation, it is easy to forget this and make a mistake without even realizing that you have erred. Again, this relates to the Self-Other divide. If you are confident and relaxed, then you will be in a better position to be sensitive to the differences of another person and adjust your own behavior accordingly. Sensitivity is useful whenever you are in a situation where you have to pay attention to anything other than your own inner dialogues, whether the 'other' be people, animals, ecosystems, or spirits. The sensitive are the ones who survive.

A very practical way in which sensitivity can be developed is to cultivate a danger-sense. You might have this sense already, particularly if you are given to wandering around dangerous neighbourhoods in inner cities. All too often, we may experience this inner 'warning' and dismiss it, as there may be no logical or rational reason that will uphold the 'scent' of danger. In my own experience I have found that ignoring the prickings of my danger sense is a mistake. This can apply not only to situations but to people. This latter is more complex. If you have a sudden perception that someone you have just met is going to be 'trouble' it can be very difficult to act on that basis, when there is no explanation to support it, but I have always found that it is a mistake not to. The danger-sense often has an element of prescience to it—the danger may not be immediately present— but it's out there waiting. If you pay attention to your danger-sense and learn to trust it, then you will find that at times it expands, becoming an aura of expectation—a foreshadowing, that something is about to happen. Such sensitivity is an achievement—it arises as a byproduct of your discipline and awareness. Don't try to explain it or force it to be there, just listen to it. It might save your, or someone else's life. A friend of mine was on a bus with his girlfriend on their way home from a party. Suddenly they both had the feeling that something undefinable was 'wrong'—and so they did not get off the bus at their usual stop, but at the next one. Walking back home, they passed their usual dropping point, only to find that two cars had collided nearby and flattened the stop sign. Had they left the bus at that point, they could have been killed when the cars collided.

CHAPTER FOUR

ANOTHER CRACK IN THE WALL

A key feature of contemporary approaches to magic is the use and exploration of practical techniques, the aim of which is to bring about changes in perception, attitude, and widen our possibilities for action. This requires the development of particular abilities and skills which form the foundations for further work. The old saying that "you cannot run before you can walk" is particularly apt when it comes to magic, where it is necessary to be able to develop particular skills before one can make the most effective use of techniques which require them. A very basic example of this is just sitting still. If you are unable to sit still and silent, you will not have much success with any magical technique which requires, at the very least, that you sit still.

Many core magical 'training' exercises seem trivial or boring. Most of us would probably prefer to do something stimulating and varied rather than sitting in an awkward posture doing nothing. In a way, part of the rationale for such an exercise *is* that it is boring or seemingly difficult. Such exercises are a way of testing the limits of your Achievable Reality. You are challenging your inherent resistance to the possibility of change, and widening the cracks in the facade of paramount reality.

D.R.A.T

The keys to becoming a magician are relatively simple. So simple in fact, that people tend to overlook them in search of complex systems of belief and abstraction. An example of such simplicity is the DRAT formula for action:

D—Discipline
R—Relaxation
A—Attention
T—Transformation

Without discipline we would not learn. Without discipline we probably wouldn't get up out of bed in the morning. We need discipline to conquer our greatest magical adversary—inertia, which tends to appear in the form of little voices which sway our resolve by arguing that what can be done right now can easily be put off until tomorrow. Yet, while a little discipline helps spur us onwards, too much discipline can actually lead us back into inertia, particularly if the goals we set for ourselves are unrealistic. So discipline requires Relaxation if it is to be used well. It is possible to be both relaxed and disciplined simultaneously. For discipline to be effective, we have to be relaxed about it, and within it. If we are to be disciplined and relaxed, then we also need to be Attentive. Attention is a skill. It is difficult to be attentive to what is happening around us; it is hard to be attentive to our own bodily sensations, behavioral habits, and attitudes. It is very difficult to be attentive of many things simultaneously. To be attentive requires Discipline and Relaxation. Transformation is the synthesis and outcome of the other three qualities. If we are disciplined, then we transform ourselves. If we are relaxed, we transform ourselves, and if we are attentive, we transform ourselves. Transformation, of course, requires Discipline, Relaxation and Attention.

DRAT can be applied within a wide variety of life situations, but is particularly useful when learning new skills and abilities which require practice and repetition. A good deal of magical training is the learning of new skills and abilities which are applied, at first, within a ritual space. However, it is a limitation to be competent and confident only within a ritual space. The trick is to be able to apply these skills and techniques into wider and wider areas of one's experience, until magic becomes not so much something that you do occasionally, but a set of principles for dealing with the world through which you move.

BODYMIND TRAINING

Relaxation is itself a good starting-point for magical training, particularly as to relax, you have to be aware of your body. There is a great tendency to forget the body and live 'inside' one's thoughts, to the level where we feel that the body is something which carries our minds around. Western approaches to magic have, over the last few decades, become very cerebral and abstract. Relaxation is a good counter exercise for this. Also, learning the ability to relax can be seen as the beginnings of Sorcery—as an act of willing a change in one's reality. Relaxation technique rests on the skill of uniting thought, breath, and action. On a very practical level it requires that we understand the relationship between thoughts, feelings, and physiological changes in the body.

Through the course of each day we tend to experience stresses of one kind or another. Our responses to stress are very individual—some people enjoy a level of stress that others would find difficult to cope with. Our ability to cope with stress factors changes according to environmental fluctuations. Stress factors are also cumulative, and the general response to stress overload is to trigger the flight-fight response: the Liver releases stored glucose into the bloodstream, the heart pumps faster, muscles prepare of action, and the digestive system shuts down. If the body is geared up for flight or fight, but there is no possibility of physical or psychological resolution, chronic problems can develop. For example, muscle tension can develop into headaches and pains. A further problem is that often, we do not modify our expectations about what we can *realistically* achieve, even when we are no longer operating at peak performance. This is known as Performance Dissonance. There is a gap between what we think we can do, and what can actually be done. The struggle to meet unrealistic expectations reinforces feelings of anxiety and low self-esteem, which of course places more stress on the BodyMind.

To be able to relax effectively then, requires the ability to identify the symptoms of stress. Secondly, you have to examine your habits and attitude and ask yourself are they likely to reduce stress or increase it? You must be prepared to change factors in your environment, your lifestyle, and your habits. You must also be prepared to accept that some factors will be beyond your control, and must be dealt with by other approaches.

Anxiety has three interrelated components which form an anxiety loop. Firstly, Stress factors give rise to physiological arousal. (Thought: "Oh No! I get really upset when this happens"). Secondly, this arousal is interpreted as anxiety. (Thought "Just as I thought! I'm getting anxious!"). Thirdly, the identification of the physiological arousal as anxiety triggers

Negative Self-Statements. ("I'm going to faint/be sick/cause a scene"). Which of course tends to lead to further stress.

So how can this anxiety loop be broken? Again, effective relaxation requires three components. Firstly, there is the physical. Learning to breathe deeply and easily, applying the simple breathing techniques of basic meditation techniques is excellent, as are patterns of muscle relaxation. Secondly, there is the Cognitive element. This relates to thoughts and feelings which arise out of physiological changes. It is necessary to be able to identify these habituated thoughts and change them. Much has been written in the new age movement about 'positive thinking' and affirmations, and these concepts should not be discounted. It is all too common for us to deliberately invoke anxiety by visualising a potentially stressful situation and anticipating all the things which could go horribly wrong, and thus prepare for a situation by worrying about it. Self-affirming thoughts reduce stress. Equally, when anticipating a potentially difficult situation, it is more effective to visualise yourself making a realistic assessment of the situation, trying out suitable approaches and considering possible alternatives. Acting out or rehearsing by visualisation tends to make the real thing less awesome. Thirdly, there is the Behavioral element. The ways in which we respond in stressful situations are often inadequate or inappropriate. Being able to relax means that we use the skill in a wide variety of situations, and also evaluate other behaviors and change them. A good example of behavioral modification is to be aware of unnecessary tensions, and eliminate them. The steps to relaxation outlined above have much in common with other, more 'magical' skills. As a core magical technique, relaxation is very much about bringing about "a change in accordance with will," yet even such a seemingly basic change can have wider ramifications. The relevance of Relaxation to magic has already been discussed in relation to Confidence. It is also highly relevant to the practice of Sorcery. Body Awareness Relaxation training demonstrates how much of our bodily experience we block out of consciousness. As a simple exercise in widening body awareness, attempt to focus your attention onto distinct areas of your body. It is very easy to start this when you are completely relaxed—focusing awareness into your fingertips or your toes. You can also try this exercise anywhere. If, for example, you are standing up, and very aware of your aching feet, try and move your awareness to your armpit or the backs of your knees. You can develop this exercise further by attempting to cast your awareness behind your back, or across as much of your body surface as possible.

POSTURAL SHIFTS

Examine the way your posture makes you feel. Do you habitually slouch, stoop, swagger? Try different ways of walking: cocky, casual, manic, sexy. Apply the knowledge you gain to your magical practice. Also, be aware of any habitual seating patterns that you have. Be aware of your own body-language with regard to other people. See if you can discover your own postural habits, and then try some others out. Does this lead to any changes in your behavior? Try adopting the body language which you feel is appropriate to qualities which you wish to develop. It is also useful to be attentive of how other people respond to postural changes. As a development of this exercise, try keeping your posture upright and relaxed (not easy—try t'ai chi or the Alexander Technique if you have problems). Then try leading with different parts of the body. Don't stick them out, just imagine you are being gently pulled along by the part in question. Good ones to try are groin, belly, chest, nose and forehead. Forget everything you've read about chakras and examine your own feelings.

DO EASY

As an extension of relaxation training, examine any action that you make, no matter how simple, and find the *easiest* way of doing it. Apply this method to everyday actions—dressing, undressing, picking up objects, performing routine tasks. You will find yourself expending much less energy, and being aware of what you are doing, rather than 'rushing' through a task while your thoughts are projecting into a future beyond the task. When you touch something, pay attention to the brush of your fingers upon it, feel the object through your fingers and move it with just the right amount of energy. Look at objects with a cool appraisal and visualise what you want to do with it and find the easiest way to do it.

Do Easy exercises demonstrate how we classify tasks as boring or routine, acts to be stumbled through as we project ourselves into a more interesting future. Direct the attention into actions that we usually think are unworthy of consideration; opening a door, picking up a glass, slicing bread. There is an Easy way to Do everything and anything. We are unusually unaware of performing simple tasks until something happens which hampers us. How would losing an arm affect your everyday life?

MOVING IN TIME

Although we experience Time as a separate dimension, it is in actuality a byproduct of Consciousness. We are constantly moving backwards and forwards in terms of experienced Past (memory) and anticipated futures (fantasy). Although much of magical practice is concerned with the ability to remain in the *immediate present,* it is also useful to be able to make use of our personal Past and Futures.

Remembering significant instances, nostalgia, or reliving events from our past triggers emotions and physiological changes. To do this requires the ability to assemble a gestalt of sensory memories. For example, bring back the memory of a former lover. Replay a moment of eye-contact and feel the shadow-shock of your excitatory response. Recall the sensation of a caress, the ghost of a voice, the thumping of your heart. Allow your feelings to intensify and be aware of bodily sensations. This 'evocation' of emotion through memory has numerous applications. For example, if you have 'unfinished business' with someone out of your past, you can evoke them and enter a dialogue. Another use of this technique is to bring forth an intense emotion and then allow the trigger source to fade, while intensifying the emotion, so that it is freed of identifications. This 'free' emotion can then be used for further acts of magic. We move forward in time using fantasy, anticipating and rehearsing situations according to emotion and expectation. If you are depressed, then you will tend to slide into a future wherein all your fears and worst-case scenarios have prominence. Fantasy becomes a form of selective feedback, reinforcing and reflecting thoughts until we 'convince' ourselves of the momentary "rightness" of an intention. Similarly, we create fantasies which effectively create a vision of a 'future' space that we are moving towards, but that is always, somehow, out of reach. In occult systems of belief, this tendency manifests in terms of the New Age, Age of Aquarius, Aeon of Horus, Chaos, Bugs Bunny or whoever/whatever you like. When there is an idealised future projection that we are working towards, it will remain forever just out of reach. The Great Work of Magic is the collapsing of the future into the immediate present; the magician seizes reality and lives *now,* free from the bonds of his past, and knowing that the future is the manifestation of his Will.

Exploring and understanding one's relationship with Time is a basic requisite of magical practice. At a basic level, this involves the observance of shifts in awareness and perception according to seasonal and diurnal cycles. We tend to think of ourselves as unchanging, despite the time of the day and the season of the year, but these can have very subtle effects on us. Observe, understand, and make the best possible use of your fluctuations in perception. There is no single, objective Time which is 'out there' distinct from us, and underlying our 'natural' experience, there are hidden depths of complexity and ambiguity.

LATERAL DIARIES

As an extension of the magical diary experiment with a record divided into four columns. In the first column record the physical elements of a journey or situation. In the second column record any memories which arose during this time. In the third column record any fragments of reading—phrases from a book, newspaper or advertisement, and in the fourth, any snatches of conversation you may have overheard. This practice will demonstrate the non-linear connections between events that we often censor from awareness.

SHADES OF PERCEPTION

Once you begin to go look behind the scenes of 'normal' experience, there is no stopping. Just as we tend to experience Time as an objective dimension, we tend to think of perception as something passive, a bridge between the internal 'I' and the world beyond. Yet perception is dynamic; it fluctuates and changes according to mood, environment and cognition. There are two basic approaches to exploring perception, which may be characterised as narrowing and widening.

SENSORY ENHANCEMENT

The first approach involves the exploration of each sensory modality in turn. *Object Concentration* is the ability to fixedly hold one's gaze on a particular object for prolonged periods of time. Some degree of proficiency at *Visualization* is a basic requirement for magical practice. Begin with simple shapes and work up to detailed scenes. Explore your relationship with colours. For example, I know that I live in a radically-different universe to many of my peers as I see colours differently. The sense of smell also plays a key role in magic. Smell is a direct hotline to memory and association. Notice how smells evoke memories and build your own correspondences between perfumes, emotions, and symbol systems for use in orchestrating experiences. Extend your ability to hear sounds by focusing on different elements of sound. Spend a week listening to the pitch of people's voices. Is there a difference between *what* people say and *how* they say it? Explore the sense of touch by being aware of all objects and fabrics. Explore surfaces with your eyes closed. Instead of reading or talking at the same time that you are eating, let the taste of food dominate your awareness. Eat a slice of lemon and then, a couple of days later, evoke the memory of the act.

There are numerous magical programmes of exercises designed to explore the senses in turn, but it is just as easy, and more fun to make your own up.

PERCEPTUAL GESTALTS

Although we tend to isolate each sensory modality, our actual experience is that of a gestalt (whole). I am writing this sentence, eating a biscuit, aware of the chair against my body, listening to cars pass outside the window and aware of the room temperature. Although the imaginative faculty tends to be discussed as primarily visual, we can also, of course, evoke tastes, proprio-ceptive (pressure, temperature), kinesthetic actions (orientation of the body in space), smell, sounds, and tastes. If for example, you wished to imagine yourself paddling in water, you could assemble a perceptual gestalt which combined visualisation of yourself in the scene, the feeling of your feet being in water, the motion of the water against your legs, an appropriate smell, feeling of sun against your back, and a soundtrack.

Assembling, and therefore creating such scenes constitutes the basis of what is known as *Pathworking.* In this form, the magician constructs a narrative with a mythic or instructive subtext into which he steps, identifying with the experience to such an extent that it becomes personally meaningful. The assemblage of imagery can be undertaken consciously or can occur spontaneously as the mind has an amazing capacity for constructing complex scenes using very little information.

There are generally, three types of Pathworking: Structured, Semi-structured, and Unstructured. An example of a Structured Pathworking is given in Chapter Seven. These Pathworkings are complete narratives, providing perceptual, emotional and behavioral cues, which the user simply follows passively. These Pathworkings are especially useful as training exercises, particularly when you are beginning to work with a belief-system with which you are unfamiliar. These Pathworkings are useful if read onto audio tape, or, as is more usual, read by another person.

Semi-structured Pathworkings have less detail. They tend to begin with an 'entrance sequence' which sets up the place or zone which is to be explored, and what the point of you being there is, after which you are left to your own devices. For example, the narrator leads you to a strange castle, giving you enough perceptual cues to build the imagery, and then tells you that you must look for someone who will give you a 'key' to your own magical power. After which, you're on your own. This approach gives you more freedom of movement and creativity within the exercise.

Unstructured, or spontaneous Pathworkings may consist of a single three-dimension image, such as a tarot card, or even a rune or I Ching hexagram. The idea here is to use the symbol or image as a doorway or gate, and to project yourself through it into a mythic landscape which lies beyond it.

What can Pathworkings be used for? Apart from training and belief-system familiarisation, one of the basic uses is to place you into a situation which triggers emotional and cognitive reactions to the level when you identify completely with what is happening. A Pathworking in which you die, are buried and go through the various stages of decomposition will, if nothing else, remind you of the inevitability of death, and perhaps help you work on your fear of death. Pathworkings can also be designed which have 'free areas' for scrying, talking to entities, or performing enchantments.

KINESTHETIC MEMORY

Awareness of our orientation in space, and of how muscular movements combine in movement can be used to heighten awareness of what is generally called the Body of Light, Astral Body or Double. Raise your left arm slowly, being aware of changes in muscles, the slight air resistance, and the movement of the joints and bones. Do this a few times, and then vividly evoke those sensations, while imagining that you are raising your left arm. Try this until you can experience raising your 'kinesthetic' left arm almost as vividly as raising your 'real' left arm. If you continue to try this practice with a range of body movements and orientations, you will find eventually that you can move freely around in this body. The Double has a great deal of magical applications. It can be used to 'rehearse' potentially difficult situations or tasks (as an extension of relaxation and Do Easy). It can also be used in shape-shifting and invocation (see Chapter Eight) and also in the exploration of dream and liminal trances.

THE ASTRAL TEMPLE

Building an astral temple combines elements of perceptual gestalts and the use of Kinesthetic memory. The astral temple is where you 'go', using your imagination, to perform acts of magic. Traditional descriptions of astral temples make much use of quasi-Masonic and hermetic symbolism, but there is no reason why you cannot develop your own temple using symbolism and background ideas which you feel to be more appropriate, such as a cyberspace zone, space station or skyscraper. The astral temple can be used for all works of magic that you would normally do on the 'physical,' and as a starting point for exploration of inner worlds and landscapes. This is a realm where the only limit is the span of your imagination. With practice you can build into it emotional associations so that, whenever you enter it, you become calm, relaxed, and feel yourself at your most powerful.

THE STAR CHAMBER

The Star Chamber is sphere of transparent crystal suspended in deep space. Its dimensions are capable of being enlarged to suit different requirements. To enter the Star Chamber, visualise the eight-rayed chaos star whirling in front of you, so that it becomes a whirling vortex, which draws you into the chamber. In the centre of the chamber is a crystalline pillar, set at waist height. If you place your hands on the pillar, the Chamber shimmers with a brief flash of purple light, and you have full control of its functions. The Star Chamber is both an astral temple and a vehicle for traveling through the multiverse. You can move to any point in time-space by placing your hands on the control pillar and asserting your will. You can also extrude various devices from the walls of the chamber to perform different tasks—globes for scrying and generating Servitors, bizarre energy projectors for the projection of desires, or baffles and collectors for collecting the radiation of black holes.

TRANCE AND PERCEPTION

We shift in and out of different shades of perception continuously throughout each day; daydreaming, fantasy, concentrating on a difficult task, listening to music, becoming absorbed in a situation so that background noises disappear. When we talk of entering trance, we are referring to a deliberate or intentional act of altering perception according to specific parameters. In modern Western Society we tend to have very fixed ideas about what constitutes a trance state—we tend to think of someone who is passive, eyes closed and limp, or oblivious to their surroundings. We tend to think of hypnotised people (the word hypnosis derives from Hypnos—Greek god of sleep) as quiescent and awaiting instructions. The term 'trance' is often understood as a state of profound absorption which fills one's awareness completely. The ability to enter and prolong such states at will is another prime requisite for magical living.

There are many routes into trance, most of which can be classified as Excitatory or Inhibitory techniques. Excitatory techniques, such as hyperventilation, dancing, chanting, drumming or any other strong stimulation, when prolonged, have distinct physiological effects, and enable the magician to attain an ecstatic peak wherein awareness of anything other what is held in the mind as a projection of will collapses. It is at such moments that spells may be cast, the persona of a god may take shape and voice, or beliefs embedded in the Deep (unconscious) Mind. Inhibitory techniques serve to silence the internal dialogue, confuse linear time-sense and disturb the boundaries of the ego-sense through sensory deprivation, sleeplessness, fasting, or slow, rhythmic breathing. All these techniques have distinct physiological effects, and demonstrate that physical awareness is a prime necessity for magic. A problem that we acquire from our culture is that we tend to be very 'head-oriented' in our experience—caught up with the continual commentary of the inner dialogue, and the words and images of the Hyper-real. Our sense of being a stable personality is maintained by transactions, both real and imaginary, with others. Move somewhere isolated and the self becomes more malleable—another classical magical gambit for entering trance states. The personality we acquire sets the limits on what we can, and cannot do. Often, by entering trance states, whether intentionally or not, we can perform feats or tasks that are normally outside our normal repertoire. If the self-referential awareness is frozen by shock, or distracted, the body seems to take over, moving us out of the way of danger. We like to think of ourselves as being 'in control' of our bodies. This is in itself a problem, as 'letting go' and becoming disinhibited (especially in a group setting) is very difficult for some of us—letting it all hang out is generally frowned upon. In other cultures, however, disinhibition is sanctioned and is the mark of a successful event. Here's Lucian's description of a Priestess of Delphi entering trance:

> She went blundering frantically about the shrine, with the god mounted on the nape of her neck, knocking over the tripods that stood in her path. The hair rose on her scalp, and when she tossed her head the wreaths went flying over the bare floor...her mouth foamed frenziedly; she groaned, gasped, uttered weird sounds, and made the huge cave re-echo with her dismal shrieks. In the end, Apollo forced her to intelligible speech.

Entering trance is not always a pleasant experience, particularly trance states involving possession. The feeling that something else is using your limbs, and that your voice is not your own, is very odd. The natural tendency, especially for Westerners, is to resist the experience, even when the incoming spirit is a beneficent one. Often, people who are possessed have no memory or awareness of what happened to them. Magicians have, over the ages, resorted to drugs, physical exertion or prolonged ritual to temporarily blot out the personality, making possession easier.

WHY ENTER TRANCE STATES?

Here are some good reasons:

1) Knowledge (i.e., that which cannot be gained in other ways). This ranges from asking auntie Freda what's it like on the other side, to asking a specific question about herbs to a particular healing spirit. This can sometimes involve journeying to particular parts of the innerworlds to consult with a particular entity.

2) Enhancement of Abilities. Possession by a war-god enhances martial prowess, or temporary authority over other spirits. For example, I had a client who had a recurring throat problem. I examined her in a light 'vision' trance and saw a toad-like creature that had swelled itself up and lodged in her throat. No way was it going to come out willingly. My allies advised me (again in trance) that the only entity the spirit would take notice of was an even bigger toad, so we performed a healing ceremony during which I became possessed by a toad-spirit, in order to interact with the one in my clients' throat.

3) Communal Ecstasy. The magician provides a very important task for tribe or community—mediating between the everyday world and the larger-than-life world of myth and communal lore. The magician becomes, or allows others to become involved in sacred mythic participation acting as the guide—navigating the secret paths of the community's cosmology. This brings up one of the biggest stumbling blocks to assuming magical roles in our culture—the fact that Western society has an extremely complex pool of mythic images to draw upon. This is not to belittle the magical innerworlds. For example, a Tamang Shaman of Tibet participates in a mythic world shared by other members of the community—its history, myth and accumulated stories—actualised and intensified by years of training, visions, and rites. Contrast this with the mythic world available to someone in modern Britain—an island that has been for centuries a melting-pot of many different cultures, with the electronic arms of the videodrome bringing in information from all over the planet, across both distance and time. It is possible for someone to have a good academic grasp of Tamang shamanistic beliefs, not to mention SF, fantasy, mythology, upbringing and the myriad ways of expressing spiritual endeavours. Also, modern society has tended to hand over the realm of the mythic to professionals: therapists, entertainers, philosophers—and we are to a large extent, cut off from participation in the mythic world, except (for the most part), sanctioned and sanitised escape routes which support consensus reality even as they provide the illusion that they challenge it. Anyway, all this leads to a pretty complicated mythic life. Fortunately, some mythic images and processes, such as the Underworld Journey are fairly universal. Others however, become 'lost' as people forget or garble the routes into experiencing/understanding them. We rely so much on 'secondhand daylight'—reading and watching other people's experience—that the oral transmission of knowledge is comparatively rare. The first Witch Coven I was involved with set a good standard—whenever the priestess wanted to impart the 'feel' of magic, we would go out into the open—a park, moon-lit street or the sea shore. Direct, physical experience, especially when accompanied by a guide who isn't into fucking you over, is better than sitting indoors reading a book any day! Anyhow, I digress.

4) Connectivity. This is concerned with making connections — finding links between different ideas and subjects; making a creative leap that brings on a flood of new ideas and enthusiasm. I often enter a trance state to overcome writer's block—letting fragments of conversation, poetry or images slip across my inner eye. Something will well up from the inside, and ideas and connections leap up like iron filings onto a magnet.

5) Demonstration of Ability. In our culture, you may be able to get away with impressing people as a magician because you've plowed through the complete works of Aleister Crowley (no mean feat!). Apprentice magicians however, are sometimes required to enter trance states as a demonstration of their prowess. It is quite common for spirits to test you by placing you under extreme psychic pressure, so that the experience becomes a compressed version of the underworld initiation. Some spirits, demons, and deities will do their best to drive you bananas, only yielding their wisdom when you have proved yourself equal to the task. The spirits of psychotropics are particularly prone to that kind of behavior.

You can't become a magician in isolation from everyone else, although periods of deliberate isolation are necessary from time to time. Also, there aren't many instructors in magic hanging about (not unless you commit yourself to an endless round of weekend workshops), so you will have to learn from everyone and everything. It's important to learn to recognise the onset of changes in awareness, and explore all possible routes into trance. Learn to trust your own senses and your intuition, rather than the internal dialogue or what you think you "ought" to do.

Again, these techniques serve to free awareness from the limitations of linear perception and solar time. Stare into a mirror, gazing at your reflection, until the mirror darkens and you feel yourself sliding into the mirror. At first this may seen agonisingly difficult due to the ego's requirement of knowing how much Time has passed. The ego needs a sense of time passing to keep itself together as a 'fixed' entity. Any technique which serves to disturb linear awareness and the internal dialogue moves the magician into so-called Liminal Perception.

Liminal perception is a borderline state of awareness. One route into this perceptual state is the half-awake, half-dreaming condition that often results from physical exhaustion. Images or sounds arise into awareness, seemingly from 'elsewhere,' beyond the one's volition. A useful technique for becoming proficient at entering this state is scrying.

SCRYING

Scrying is a basic divinatory technique which is useful for exploring liminal perception. It can be performed using any reflective surface, such as a mirror, preferably a shiny black surface, or a bowl filled with dark fluid. Scrying requires that you be able to enter a light trance state where images arise in your mind, rather like day-dream visions, or the pictures that you see before falling asleep. The 'trick' of scrying is to try and relax, and let any images appear before you, gazing steadily into the medium that you are using, without staring too hard or intensely concentrating. This only comes with practice. At first it should be enough to let random images well up, and later on to try and answer specific questions. The area in which you are practicing should be dimly lit, and lights (candles are excellent, being less harsh than electric lights) placed so that they do not reflect in the medium you are using. Incense can also be a useful aid, particularly those resins and oils which act as relaxants. You may find it useful to perform a meditation or relaxation exercise prior to attempting to scry. Divinatory techniques such as these help develop the intuitive and psychic faculties, and the trick of relaxing and letting images arise in your mind is also a key to other talents such as psychometry and aura reading. Once you have tried the basic method, then regular practice will help you develop it. Mirror and crystal gazing is a strong magical tradition, occurring in shamanic cultures from the Americas to Africa, medieval Europe and ancient Greece. Not only have mirrors and crystals been used to divine the future, but also to communicate with ancestral spirits. Occasionally people experience scenes or entities leaving the reflective surface and merge with the surrounding environment.

DYNAMIC DREAMING

Exploring the possibilities of Dream Magic is a powerful and effective way of breaking away from linear consciousness and allowing magic *into* your life. Prospective magicians may even be identified by virtue of the content of their dreams, and it is not unusual for people to meet their guides in dreams. We tend to think of dreams as a very personal aspect of our experience, so it is sometimes disconcerting when someone that we know appears in our dreams. In dreams, historical time is abolished, and distance is no object. We may witness events from the past, future, or alternative presents.

Dreams are a useful starting point for entering the innerworlds. It can be useful to induce prophetic dreams, or meetings with spirits so that you can discuss a particular problem. A friend of mine who makes incense and perfumes reports that she occasionally dreams of a unique smell, which on waking, she can then analyse and manufacture. The magical artist Austin Osman Spare wrote that he would sometimes awake to find himself standing in front of a finished picture, having drawn it in his sleep.

KEEPING A DREAM DIARY

The first step to exploring dream magic is to keep a record of your dreams, which should be, if possible, updated as soon as you awake. Over time, keeping a record of your dreams enhances your ability to recall them in greater and greater detail. It is also invaluable for checking out the degree of confluence between dream imagery and waking experience. Keeping a dream diary will also enable you to identify recurrent symbols, images and situations which appear in your dreams, and can form the basis for willed exploration of astral zones or magic done while you are awake, based on dream imagery.

BASIC DREAM CONTROL

It is remarkably easy to make the content of dreams conform to expectation. People who are undergoing Freudian analysis tend to have 'Freudian' dreams, while people who are undergoing Jungian psychotherapy will tend to experience 'Jungian' dreams. You might choose to begin experimenting with Dream Control by setting a 'theme' for your dreams—such as a particular subject, location, or person. There are several different approaches to intentionally guiding dream content. Firstly, prior to sleep, perform a relaxation exercise and clearly formulate the Statement of Intent with regard to your dream-experience. For example, "It is my will to dream of my father." Once this is done, you can allow your mind to 'wander' until you fall asleep. Alternatively, you could try visualising a scene or image as you fall asleep. This need not be a strong visualisation, just the subject of attention as you fall asleep.

A third way of willing dream-content is to use a graphic or mantric sigil, using the techniques explained in Chapter Five. Whatever technique you use, remember that the point is not to impose your will into your dreams, but to be relaxed at the same time as formulating your intention.

DREAM TELEPATHY

The possibility of transmission of telepathic information into dreams has been the subject of a good deal of para-psychological research, usually in the form that a "sender" attempts to project some kind of information to a dreamer. However, it can happen that you will have a dream about someone in a particular situation, which they do experience. Of course, the only way that you can find out whether a not a dream had telepathic content is to check out the person(s) concerned and find out if your dream has any meaning for them. Another possibility is to establish a telepathic link between yourself and another person by using smell. If two people use a particular fragrance or perfume, to the extent that the scent of it evokes the image or memory of the other person, then this can be used to create a dream-link. If the scent is inhaled prior to sleep, while relaxed and formulating an image of the other person, and a Statement of Intent for the dream, then it is possible that the other person can experience that smell in their dream, and be more receptive to telepathic experience. I have used this technique in a series of experiments, where a partner and I found that we could awaken each other during a pre-arranged hour of the night, by using scent as a telepathic signal 'booster'.

SHARED DREAMS

A shared dream is an event wherein two or more people experience the same dream, or elements of a similar dream. Alternatively, you might dream about yourself and another person in a dream, and find out later that they too dreamt about you with them, perhaps in a different context. Again, the only way to validate this is to inform the people concerned. Attempts to orchestrate group shared-dreams can be an interesting exercise, perhaps using a semi-structured Pathworking to provide the basic setting which participants could later attempt to dream themselves to.

DREAMING THE FUTURE

That dreams have the power to warn us of the future is an ancient idea, and precognitive dreams played an important role in ancient civilisations. On the basis of a dream, the destiny of a country or state could be shaped. Dreams about the future can be symbolic, distorted, or even highly detailed and clear, but it is often difficult beforehand to distinguish the important elements of the dream. A few years ago, some friends of mine decided to undertake an experiment in dreaming the future. They planned a visit to a town that none of them had ever visited before, and then attempted to dream themselves there. One person kept seeing the image of a long-necked cat, but for the life of him couldn't figure out how this was relevant. When he actually visited the town, almost the first thing he saw after getting out of the car was an antique shop. In the window was a glazed model of a long-necked cat.

LUCID DREAMS

Lucidity in dreaming is the point where you realise that you are dreaming, and so no longer experience the dream passively, but can change it. Moments of lucidity can be triggered by different things. For example, I once dreamed that I was in a house which I had not lived in for over a decade. The dream was perfect in every detail, except that when I looked down at my feet, I saw that I was wearing a pair of shoes that I did not possess at that time. This incongruity jarred me into realising that I was dreaming. Lucidity can also be triggered by recognising dream elements. It is not uncommon for people to become lucid in a dream when they realise that they have had the dream before, can remember how it develops, and do not want to re-experience it. People tend to experience moments or flashes of lucidity within dreams, but it is of course possible to extent this facility, enabling you to direct the content of the dream for magical purposes. Lucidity can be brought about using suggestion while awake, or rather obliquely, by metaprogramming oneself so that if a particular image or scene appears, this will trigger lucidity, i.e., "I will become lucid whenever I see a yellow sphere floating towards me." The sphere could be directed by another person, or act as a Servitor (see Chapter Six) designed to trigger lucid dreaming. It can be rewarding to approach dreaming from a non-western point of view, such as that of the Australasian Aborigines or the Senoi of Malaysia. Some anthropologists believe that the Senoi dream psychology is the source of the tranquillity of their lives. When first contacted by Westerners in the 1930's, the Senoi had had no violent crime or conflicts within their community for some two to three hundred years.

AXIS MUNDI

The *Axis Mundi* is the central axis which unites all zones of experience and states of consciousness. It has many symbolic representations, such as the World Tree, Sacred Mountain, pole or Crossroads which is the centre of the magician's universe. It is not so much a place, but a matter of how you 'place' yourself. To be relaxed in the present means that you are at the "centre" of your magical reality. The act of centering yourself can take the form of an elaborate banishing ritual or a moment of no-mind relaxation before you begin a task. The core elements of centering are simple:

1. Giving attention to your physical presence.

2. Establishing the gates, cardinal points or dimensions (according to your chosen scheme of representation) of which you are at the centre).

3. Self-identification with a chosen source of inspiration— merging the macrocosm (total experience) with the microcosm (self). An example of an orthodox Banishing Ritual is given in Chapter Six. It is useful to find a range of exercises which will serve in a variety of situations. Centering exercises should give rise to a feeling of relaxation and being prepared and poised for action. These can range from elaborate banishings which are used as preparation for intense ritual work, to simply exercises which can be used anywhere, at a moment's notice.

The *Axis Mundi* may also be considered the access point to the different innerworlds of the mythic cosmology. It seems reasonable to assume that the Qabalistic Tree of Life evolved from a shamanic world-tree. The crossroads is another *Axis Mundi* symbol, appearing in Celtic, Greek, and Haitian mythologies. The innerworlds are populated by hosts of spirits, demons and ancestors. Contact and knowledge of these entities is part of the shared totality of experience of a tribal society, mediated by the shaman. This is rarely the case in Western culture—there is a vast variety of innerworlds which may be explored. The Deep Mind is very receptive to suggestion (after all, that's how we learn), and can clothe itself in any kind of images. Using the astral temple and body formation techniques discussed earlier, you can explore any magical innerworld, from the mythic landscapes of the Norse Gods to the pristine gardens which can be entered through the Chinese I Ching trigrams.

THE MAGICAL WILL

Consciousness arises from perception, which arises from our direct engagement with the environment. The Will can be similarly understood as the engagement of intentionality along a given vector. When you say "It is my Will to..." you are projecting into the future. The Magical Will should not be confused with so-called will-power or concentration. It is useless to set yourself stringent tests, oaths or promises, as if the desire to overcome a habit or behavior is weaker than the desire to maintain it, then you will surely fail, and thus reinforce your sense of being weak.

The keys to the Will are in relaxation in the present, unity of desire and unity of purpose. As you will see in the next chapter, proficiency at Sorcery requires that you can isolate, identify and focus upon specific desires, while at the same time, become detached from them. Desires manifest when they have been isolated, exteriorised and then forgotten. Acts of ritual magic, which involve the orchestration of perception and action along a directional vector, serve as exercises in unity of purpose. For example, I project forth an intent: I visualise the sigil which is my desire. I slowly push my hand forwards, as though the air is resisting its movement. At the same time, I visualise a beam of energy leaping forth from my hand. I exhale with a cry of "Kia!" All these actions are united in the single purpose of projection into the future. Thought, word and deed are one. To do your Will requires a relaxed single-mindedness of purpose, while remaining detached from the results you intend to bring about. In Zen Buddhism, this is known as 'Immovable Wisdom,' wherein one's mind is freed from attachments, of the bonds of the past, and anticipation of the future. This practice does not come easily to most of us, and it requires much patience, discipline and practice. Refinement of the Magical Will arises from practice and the constant vigilance against falling into habituated patterns of thinking and behavior. The value of simple meditation practices, such as are found in Zen practice should not be discounted, as they can be a great help in developing bodymind awareness, relaxation, and awareness of the immediate present. Many modern magicians do practice forms of martial arts, and such practices are invaluable for developing magical abilities.

CHAPTER FIVE

PLAYING WITH CHAOS

Sorcery is generally understood as the use of magical techniques and perspectives to bring about a change in one's material environment. Traditionally, the use of magical techniques for direct results has been thought of as 'Low' magic, while the quest for spiritual growth, uniting with one's 'Higher Self' or attaining transcendence from the material world was, of course, 'High' magic. This distinction perpetuated the division of the world into matter versus spirit, subjective versus objective, reflecting a general philosophy (shared by science and religion) which regarded the demands of the everyday world as being inferior to abstract metaphysics. For the Chaos Magician, such a distinction is artificial and very much a sign of self-limitation. From the Chaos perspective, Sorcery is valuable for a number of reasons. Firstly, that success with sorcery techniques embeds in one's mind the certainty that MAGIC WORKS in a way that intellectual argument or practice without clear purpose cannot. Secondly, that in working with sorcery techniques, the rigorous analysis of one's own motivations and desire-complexes is itself enlightening. Thirdly, that the practice of sorcery itself leads to considerations of personal ethics; if one is serious about bringing about change in the world, one must also accept responsibility for those changes. Moreover, bringing about change in the world tends to lead to personal changes. If I enchant for fame, then I must be able to change in order to make the best use of that fame. Fourthly, practical sorcery demands identifiable results; if I choose to enchant for Wealth, I must be able to at some point be able to say how the sorcery has contributed to my wealth. Finally, successful sorcery requires that we pay attention to the world as it is, rather than how we would like it to be. One of the great pitfalls in magical development is the tendency for people to, when the going gets tough, withdraw themselves into a safe fantasy and count themselves kings of infinite space. Sorcery, which is concerned with the everyday world, can help us keep our feet on the ground, which is very important for those who would reach for the stars.

SIGIL MAGIC

Sigil Magic, derived from the work of Austin Osman Spare has become a core sorcery technique associated with Chaos. In a way, the technique represents the basics of the Chaos approach, in that it is simple, results-oriented, and is effective regardless of one's beliefs or metaphysical speculations in general. Many of Spare's contemporaries believed that magic could not be "done" without all manner of props—robes, magical weapons, banners, altar, etc., and also that one had to be conversant in magical systems such as the Qabalah. In using sigils, Spare demonstrated that effective magic can be done at a moment's notice, virtually anywhere. Sigilisation is one of the simplest and most effective forms of results magic used by contemporary magicians. Once you have grasped the basic principles of sigilisation and experimented with some of the most popular methods of casting sigils, you can go on to experimenting with forms of sigil magic which are unique to you. The basic process of Sigil Magic can be divided into six stages, which I will explain using the acronym S.P.L.I.F.F.

S—Statement of Intent
P—Pathways available?
L—Link intent to symbolic carrier
I—Intense Gnosis/Indifferent Vacuity
F—Fire
F—Forget

STATEMENT OF INTENT

The first stage of the process is that you should get your magical intent clear—as precise as possible without, at the same time, being too overcomplicated. Vague intentions usually give rise to vague results, and the clearer the initial statement of intent is, the more likely you are to get accordant results. An acquaintance of mine once did a sigil to manifest a lover, and gave very precise details on how this paragon should look, what kind of car he should drive, etc. Needless to say, her 'desire' manifested exactly as she had specified, and she discovered too late that she had forgotten to specify 'intelligence' in her sigil, and that her 'dream lover' could only talk about himself and his car, to the extent that she found him completely boring! One of the byproducts of the process of Deconditioning discussed earlier, is that it becomes progressively easier to disentangle your own habitual patterns of thought and emotion, desires and fantasies. There is a popular idea that magicians are continually casting spells and performing rituals to bring to them all that they desire. This is a misconception of magic, and magicians tend to enchant for desires selectively and carefully, being mindful that hasty enchantments may often bring complications that were not considered beforehand, as the above example shows. Here are some techniques which can be of use when you are deciding how to deal with a desire or intent.

DIVINATION TECHNIQUES

Using a divination system can be very helpful when examining your own motivations underlying a desire. What type of system you use is very much a matter of individual taste, and Tarot, the Runes, or the I Ching seem to be the most popular. Here is an example of how divination can be useful. Shortly before writing this book, the computer which I use for writing suddenly 'crashed' to the extent that it required repair. This left me in a pathetic state which any hardened computer-user will surely sympathise with. Suddenly, the thought struck me that this would be an ideal opportunity to 'upgrade'—to buy a new system. I immediately began to try and generate strategies which would allow me to purchase a new model, without overburdening my financial resources. At the same time, I began to cast around for suitable models at a good price. I rapidly created a situation where the desire to gain a new computer was prominent in my mind for a good deal of the time. Soon, the situation became frustrating. My bank declined to loan me the money I required, and other possible routes for generating the money required were not immediate enough—I wanted a computer now! Having enmeshed myself in this tangle of desires and become frustrated and annoyed, I decided to see what my tarot cards had to say about the matter. The result was very explicit and shocking. The tarot cards pointed out that me trying to sustain a loan at the moment would have poor long-term consequences; that I really didn't need a new computer anyway, and that it would be more realistic to repair the current machine. Looking at this reading, I felt a great sense of relief and amusement at myself. This incident also gave me an insight into how we let our desires 'take control' of a situation and blind us to alternative possibilities.

If you perform divinations, you must be prepared for answers or perspectives that do not necessarily fit in with what you 'want' to see. A useful way to regard divination systems is that they are old and trusted friends—people whose views you respect and who's advice you would readily accept. By ignoring the results of a divination, you are fooling no one but yourself, demonstrating that you were not really interested in having another perspective on the situation in the first place.

S.W.O.T. ANALYSIS

The SWOT acronym stands for Strengths, Weaknesses, Opportunities, Threats. It can be useful sometimes to examine a situation, prior to taking magical action, in terms of these four points. *Strengths* refers to the strength of your position as regards the desired outcome of the intention, such as Pathways Available (see below), any information that you have access to that will strengthen your position, or anything that allows you to focus on the most appropriate factor to attempt to influence. All these things should be listed. Under *Weaknesses* you might consider possible weak areas which might interfere with the actualisation of your intent. When considering *Opportunities* look at factors such as timing—when is the optimum time to enchant for? Is there a situation which is likely to increase your chance of success? Finally, *Threats* refers to any possible negative consequences of your enchantment.

To use the SWOT analysis, first frame your general or surface Statement of intent, and then analyse it in terms of the above divisions. If you find that there are more Weaknesses and Threats to your enchantment, then it may well be wiser to consider another approach to the problem. With regard to my "I want a new computer Now!" desire, I quickly found that, when subjected to the rational SWOT procedure, that there were more Weaknesses and Threats to the success of an enchantment to bring in a large amount of money, than there were Strengths and Opportunities. Obviously, another approach was called for. In this particular instance, I cast a sigil to call forth "help" from other people, which was indeed forthcoming.

OTHER SOURCES OF INFORMATION

Apart from using divination or situational analyses, other sources of information can be useful. Asking other people their opinions, for a start. The more information you have about a situation, the greater flexibility you will have when you approach it from a magical angle. For example, I was recently approached by a third party on behalf of a client who wanted some kind of enchantment performed to meet a partner. I spent a couple of hours asking about the client's habits, social movements, personal qualities and so forth, all of which helped me to decide not only what kind of enchantment to perform, but also in what way the spell should influence matters to bring about the desired result. Performing sorcery on behalf of other people is very good for your own practice.

PATHWAYS AVAILABLE

Generally, sigils are excellent for bringing about precise, short or long-term results, which makes them excellent for works of Results Magic—healing, habit manipulation, inspiration, dream-control, and the like. It is generally considered useful if you 'open' a path for the intent to manifest along. There is a standard magical example about working for 'money' that goes along the lines of: Frater Bater does a spell for money and waits for the multiverse to provide him with the cash. In the following months he gains financially after the sudden deaths of relatives, receiving industrial compensation after falling into a combine harvester, and so on. Had he made sure that there was a possible pathway or route for the result to come in on, like writing a book (ha! ha!), applying for a new job, or entering a lottery, he might have had a better time of it. This is the way magic often works, and shows that the multiverse, if nothing else, has a slappy sense of humour.

LINK INTENT

Once you have decided upon your intent, it can then be turned into a symbolic code—a signal on which you can focus varying degrees of attention on, without recalling your initial desire. The two most common approaches to this are:

(a) Monogram—write out your intent, knock out all repeating letters, and from the rest, design a glyph.

(b) Mantra—write out intent, scramble into meaningless phrase or word, which can then be chanted. Alternatively, you could rearrange the letters of your statement of intent so that it becomes another sentence, which can be used as a mantra. For example: "I Desire Assistance in House-Hunting" could become "The Sun can Sing."

In addition to the above, you can also use other media such as smell, taste, colours, body language, and hand gestures.

INTENSE GNOSIS/INDIFFERENT VACUITY

Sigils can be projected into the multiverse via an act of Gnosis—usually, but not necessarily, within some kind of ritual/magical context. Popular routes to Gnosis include: spinning, chanting, dancing, visualisation, sensory overload or sensory deprivation, and sexual arousal. The other 'altered state' is that of Indifferent Vacuity—a sort of 'not-particularly-bothered' state. An example of sigilisation by this route is to doodle sigils while listening to a talk which is boring, but you have to take notes on.

FIRE

This is simply the projection of the sigil into the void or multiverse at the 'peak' of Gnosis/Vacuity. Examples of this include orgasm, reaching the point of blackout from hyperventilation or being asked a question about the boring talk that you were supposed to have been listening to. The projection of a sigil can, of course, be the main theme of a more-or-less orthodox magical ritual. Less orthodox methods include visualizing a sigil glyph as you feel a sneeze about to burst from your nose; or projecting a sigil at the moment when, after holding your bladder to the point where the need to urinate becomes physically painful, you let go and feel the absolute bliss of relaxation. A popular approach to empowering a sigil is during the peak of physical orgasm (or at the point where pain becomes pleasure and vice versa). As you peak into orgasm, visualise the sigil glowing brightly and then shooting off into the depths of space (photon torpedo!). If you are trying to influence a particular person, you can try imagining the sigil glowing on their chest (or whatever organ you find easiest to visualise). Note that sexual partners don't have to know what's happening—it does help though if they can give you the necessary stimulation!

FORGET

Once your sigil has been fired, you're supposed to forget the original intent and let the Butterfly Effect take its course. Forgetting what you just did can often be the hardest part of the process. It's not so bad if the intent is something you don't really care about (hence beginning with sigils for things you aren't really too attached to is a good way to begin experiments), but is more difficult if it's something you really want to happen. As long as you don't dwell on the thoughts when they arise, it shouldn't matter too much. Time for another analogy.

The ever-changing tangle of desires, wishes, fears, fantasies, etc. jostling around in our minds can be likened to a garden, albeit a somewhat unruly and overgrown one; flowers, weeds, creepers, and the occasional buried gardening rake. Going through the sigilisation process can be likened to becoming suddenly enthusiastic about tidying the garden up. You isolate one plant (i.e., your intent), separate it from the others, feed it, water it and prune it until it stands out from the rest and is clearly visible on the landscape, and then suddenly get bored with the whole job and go indoors to watch television. The trick is, next time you look at the 'garden', not to notice the plant you so recently lavished attention on.

If the intent gets tangled up with all the other stuff in your head, you tend to start projecting various fantasy outcomes— what you'll do with the money when it comes, how will it be with the boy/girl/anteater of your dreams, etc. and the desire will get run into all the others, thus decreasing the probability of it manifesting in the way you want it to.

A useful attitude to have when casting sigils is that once you've posted one off to the multiverse (which, like Santa, always gets the message), then you're sure that it's going to work, so that you don't need to expend any more effort on that particular one. Such confidence tends to arise out of having had some success with sigils previously. The result often comes about when the intent has become latent—that is to say, you've completely forgotten about it and given up on it coming about. The experience is similar to trying to hitch a lift on a deserted road in the dead of night. You've been there for hours, it's pouring down with rain and you 'know' with an air of dread certainty that no one's going to stop for you now, but you stick your thumb out anyway. What the hell, eh? Five minutes later, you get a lift from the boy/girl/anteater of two sigils back, driving a Porsche and asking you how *far* you want to go. Maddening isn't it? But sigils often seem to work out like that.

RECORDING RESULTS

If you are embarking upon a series of experiments with sigils, it can be useful to record the sigil experiment in such a way that it does not immediately bring to mind the original desire associated with the sigil. After writing up the details of your experiment, tape into your diary a scrap of paper with the sigil drawn on one side, and the original Statement of Intent penciled onto the other side.

EXPERIMENT WITH APPROACHES

In the past, I have prepared half a dozen sigils at once, then filed them and deliberately lost them. Coming across them weeks later, I have totally forgotten the original desires, and choose one at random to empower. I find repeatedly doodling a sigil when most of my attention is elsewhere can be effective. The best time I find to perform sigil magic is when I am really busy and have lots to think about, so that I don't get into the trap of thinking about the desired-for-effect. Sigils can also be incorporated into photographs, cassette recordings, video or drawings. Tattoos, ear-rings, wall-hangings and clothing designs are also possible.

LINKED SIGILS

This is a simple application of Sigil Magic technique that you can try out. Firstly prepare two Sigils—one for some desire you wish to enchant for, and the other, for something along the lines of "I will see a woman with long red hair carrying a small dog." Unless you are a particularly refined fetishist, this is something that should be fairly easy to forget. Now 'fire' this second sigil first. Prepare your other sigil and carry it around with (preferably on a small piece of paper). It might well happen, as you go about your daily affairs, that you will suddenly notice the person (or object) fitting the description you have sigilized for. At this moment, the recognition of the subject of the first sigil will slip you into a microburst of Gnosis—at this point, 'fire' your other Sigil-intense visualization of the sigil into a whirling black chaosphere (or any other preferred symbol) is one way of doing this.

SWAPPING SIGILS

It can be useful occasionally to find another person who uses Sigil Magic and to exchange sigils. This means that you have a sigil which is entirely meaningless to you and therefore, is readily forgotten. Even if someone else casts a sigil which you have compounded, then there tends to be a result in accordance with your original intent. This seems to indicate that the most important part of the whole process of sigilization is for you to frame your statement of intent and then relax 'away' from thinking about the outcome of the intent. These are the elements of the process which define the parameters of success, rather than any mysterious forces, symbolism, or magical 'energy'. This demonstrates an idea emerging within the Chaos corpus: that the explanation an individual holds for a phenomenon should not necessarily be taken as a 'true' description of what is happening, but nevertheless, that explanation generates the context by which that phenomenon takes place. In other words, the convoluted metaphysics which has grown up around much of contemporary magic provides a context of belief, within which the magician learns to relax. As discussed in Chapter Three, relaxation and confidence are keys to magical success. The role that belief plays in creating a magical context is examined in Chapter Seven.

A SORCERER'S TOYBOX

Western approaches to magic have become, over the last century or so, thoroughly pervaded by the Protestant Work Ethic. Magic is generally thought of as a serious, work-like pursuit. Indeed, magicians talk about rituals as being 'Workings'. The Chaos approach stresses that fun and pleasure are important, yet often neglected dimensions of magic. Can magic be entertaining? Play and entertainment tend to be undervalued, yet they are arguably two of the most significant of human experiences, and magic and play share common features. Both are defined in contrast to the everyday world. Both serve to draw the participant out from the ordinary world into the mythic, larger-than-life dimension. Some aspects of the magic-play perspective have been mentioned already, but play can give a useful perspective on sorcery. What is the difference between a child playing with a doll and an 'adult' sorcerer enchanting over a wax image? The sorcerer may be concentrating hard upon the enchantment. He may know all about symbolism and theories which enable him to suspend disbelief and work with the waxen image 'as if' it were his target. The child appears to be absorbed, serious, intent upon its play, but the chances are that the child finds it much easier to believe in the doll as being something other than which is immediately apparent, than the magician can invest belief in the efficacy of his wax image.

Magic has game-like aspects, yet it is rare that we can approach it on the level of being a game. It is a serious endeavour, yet it can be serious *fun*. With regard to sorcery technique, it is possible to use both a rigorous approach to structuring enchantments and a playful approach to actualising them. It's as easy as—A PIE:

Assessment

Stop. Don't do anything. Look at the situation and at all possibilities for action. Use techniques that will show you different angles or perspectives on the situation: divination, dream-oracles, asking your favourite deity or visualising various possible courses of action.

Plan

Once you have chosen a course of action. Plan what you need to do. What resources do you need? These may be magical, material, financial or the assistance of others. Do you need more information and if so, where is it going to come from?

Implementation

Now the hardest thing of all—to do it. Laziness and inertia may well intervene at this stage, which may often be the surface manifestations of fear (of failure/success). Remember, each moment of success gives more momentum to the next attempt. Each barrier breached brings a rush of pleasure and expanded possibilities.

Evaluation

We must be able to evaluate the results of our magics. To look back into the wake of your passing and be able to identify how one's will has brought about change. A key here is the ability to understand and integrate one's experiences in the light of one's magical work. The use of the Magical Diary is most important in this respect. Evaluation of the results of one's magics, and of the techniques used is often difficult, unless one is prepared to be scrupulously honest. It can sometimes become a balancing act between one's ideal manifestation of desire, and what actually occurs. For example, I once performed a sigil enchantment for "new sources of pleasure." Now I admit that underlying this intention was the hope of new sexual entanglements. Shortly after the ritual, a friend gave me some new computer game programs, which did indeed provide me with many hours of pleasure, so I was willing to count that sigil as a success. If however, I had specified a desire to be fucked senseless, and *then* had computer games turn up, I would count that enchantment as a failure. There is no all-embracing explanation for failure, although people often resort to justifications such as karma, destiny, cosmic tides or fate or even the will of the gods in order to explain 'why' it is that something hasn't happened in accordance with expectation. Oddly enough, there seems to be the implicit suggestion that when enchantments are successful, it is a reflection of one's own magical ability, but when spells go awry "it was your karma not to have that happen."

Thus the preparation and core procedures which are implicit in an act of sorcery depend upon discipline, attention and the awareness of the consequences of any resultant transformation. This leaves us with the option of being fairly relaxed over the actual implementation of sorcery technique, as a rummage through the contents of a sorcerer's toybox demonstrates.

INSIDE THE TOYBOX
Plasticines

Plasticine gives endless possibilities as a magical tool. Here is an example of enchantment with Silly-Putty. Once you have your Statement of Intent, roll the plasticine into strips and form the letters of your Statement. After meditating upon the Statement, mash the plasticine together and roll it into a ball again. Continue to shape and reshape the plasticine with your hands, while also using hyperventilation, and glossolalia. Sigils of intent can be gouged into the plasticine, shaped by rolling it, and then destroyed again. As you enter gnosis, divide the plasticine into two halves. One half is you, the other, your desire. At the climax of the ritual, mash them together. The same lump of plasticine can be kept and re-used over and over again in sorcery workings. You can add bits of your body into it (nails, hair, blood etc.).

Candles

Using candles for casting spells is a popular approach to magic that has inspired many books on the subject. You can inscribe sigils, runes and any other symbols on a candle, and leave it to burn itself down while you go off and do something else. Making Love by candlelight is magical in itself, and indeed, if you think far enough along these lines you may come up with 'magical' uses for candles which tend not to be mentioned in the spellcasting books.

String

There is much that can be done with a piece of string. Enchantment using knots is well-known within modern witchcraft revivals, as is the use of string to create webs, labyrinths, 'cats cradles' and other complicated tangles, which have spells whispered into them or have become the focus for enchantments. Braided pieces of hair can also be used as power tools, particularly if the hair was 'sacrificed' to assist in a particular goal (for example, cutting one's hair to improve job prospects). The hair of dead relatives or associates can be easily imbued with mythic power.

'Givens'

This term denotes anything which you have been given, which does not have an immediate purpose, yet is significant due to the circumstances in which you received it, or the associations which you attach to it. It becomes 'magical' due to it being a 'gift'—the sort of thing which you might never formally imbue with magical power, yet which ends up in your toybox/power bundle/altar anyway.

Found Objects

Found Objects are similar to the above, but tend to be the things that you pick up for no very good reason, and then find yourself loath to throw away. Eventually, you will find a 'use' for them. Years ago I found part of an old telephone handset. I carried it around for months, and eventually found myself 'listening' to it at odd moments. At first this was just a playful form of "weirding out" whoever I was sitting next to. By and by, I found that by make-believing that I was listening to a particular friend using the phone, she would invariably turn up within five minutes of me 'chatting' to her. Of course, the more I tried to deliberately use the phone to call her, the less likely she was to appear. Other examples of 'Found Objects' include bits of animals, odd shards of circuitry, things which are probably pieces of something bigger.

Crystals

Crystals have been much-hyped as items of almost universal magical application (depending upon what you read). Crystals have curative powers, can be used for 'safe sex', buried in the earth as gifts to mommy Gaia, used in conjunction with ley lines to contact dolphins, and their misuse has even been claimed as a deciding factor in the fall of the Atlantean Empire! On a perhaps less prosaic level, crystals can be used for Scrying. Doctor John Dee, for example, used a ball of Obsidian crystal in his magical experiments. Crystals have also, from ancient times, been used as Talismans, and any 'good' book on crystals will provide you with a list of symbolic attributions for crystals. One magical use of crystals which has been ignored by new-agers is the use of crystals as spirit traps. Again, this is a very traditional use, there being many tales of entities being lured into crystals and other types of receptacles. It is certainly possible to 'trap' an entity in a crystal, and you can also designate a crystal as a 'home' for an entity. They can be used as personal power objects and, if nothing else, they look pretty on an altar.

Dominoes And Dice

Dominoes and dice have obvious associations with games—there are also divination techniques using them.

Wood

Pieces of Wood can be useful at times. The stick from a lollipop for example, with runes or sigils added, can be used to make a nondescript talisman. The act of hammering a nail into a piece of wood can become the physical component of an act of enchantment.

Crayons 'n' Chalk

Chalk is the unsung magical tool of traditional magical approaches, which called for circles, triangles and complicated names to be laid down upon floors. Crayons, obviously, can be used in creating pictures, yantras, etc.

Pendulums

A pendulum can come in handy occasionally, especially for finding lost or hidden objects. On at least two occasions I have turned up at friends' houses to find them methodically turning the place upside-down in search of some small but apparently item. A calm scan around the room with a pendulum turned up the lost item in unexpected places. You can also use pendulums to dowse a map, or to answer simple yes/no questions. It is often useful to be able to perform acts of divination without using complex systems such as runes or tarot cards, and even tea leaves, which tend to be scorned by magicians as unworthy of contemplation, can have their uses.

Balloons

The act of blowing into a balloon can be used to project a magical intent. Alternatively, you could cast a sigil by attaching it to a balloon filled with helium, and launch it into the atmosphere. Bursting a balloon can be used to 'climax' a ritual, and of course you could use balloons in accordance with colour correspondences. The truly adept could even form them into shapes to represent fetishes or animals.

Figures

Several years ago, I had around my house a ceramic pixie figure. A souvenir from a holiday. One day, I decided that I would give this pixie the ability to 'find things' that were lost around the house. Whenever I mislaid something, I would go and ask the 'pixie' where it was, and then keep looking. After I found the lost item, I would go and thank the pixie, and sometimes put a silver coin under its base. Over time, this routine worked very well, and I persuaded other members of the household to "go ask the pixie" where they had mislaid household objects and, when they had found what they were looking for, to go and thank him. This is a very basic approach to magical evocation, and I have found over the years that the most effective way to 'feed' a spirit is to attribute any successes which relate to its sphere of operation to its action, and to develop a relationship with it.

MAGICAL WEAPONS

The above are just a few of the possibilities for using everyday objects in sorcery practice. In addition, there are the more 'formal' weapons of modern magic, being the dagger, the wand, the chalice, the pentacle and the lamp. It is possible to discourse at length on the symbolism which has grown up around each of these items, but I'm not going to, as you don't need to have digested heaps of symbolism to make effective use of them.

The Wand or Staff is a physical representation of the act of projecting one's will forth (intentionality directed along a given vector). The key to understanding the magical will is in the concept of unity of desire. Whereas the swearing of oaths, promises and abstentions serves only to set up conflicts within the mind, the magician seeks unity of desire *before* he acts, hence the importance of preparation in acts of sorcery. The wand also represents the initial drive to begin a project.

The Dagger is often used in ritual magic as an extension of one's finger. It is used to draw sigils, pentagrams and other magical symbols in the air. To the dagger is attributed the qualities of analysis and discrimination. Any magical dagger is thus only as effective as your own skill at analysis and discrimination, whether this is applied to yourself or a situation, hence the importance of planning, and breaking down a goal into its constituent steps and elements.

The Chalice is used as a physical receptacle of transmission. Thus it may be used in ritual to hold wine (or other fluid) which is first 'charged' via an act of invocation and then consumed by the celebrants, or it can be used for scrying. Thus to the chalice is attributed all techniques whereby perception is unhindered by the internal dialogue or by lust for a result, such as oracular states of consciousness, the use of tarot, dreaming, or mental silence.

The Pentacle represents the process of synthesis and is the object whereupon the results of one's magical work are made manifest and understood. In rituals, objects which are to be charged with magical power would be placed upon a pentacle.

Finally, the Lamp is the physical representation of inspiration. It often appears in the form of a light-bulb over the head of a cartoon character. In traditional western magic, the idea of Godhead or the Holy Guardian Angel are two aspects of the Lamp weapon, although it could just as easily be a 'primitive' fetish object or a symbol which, over time, one comes to associate with gnosis and inspiration.

It is important to remember that the development of the requisite qualities are more useful than the physical shells which serve to encapsulate them. There is an old adage that magical weapons should either be made by their user, given to them, or at least found in unusual ways. Equally, the act of saving money so that you can buy an item of occult equipment, especially if you have made some kind of sacrifice (such as walking to work), will also confer the association of 'specialness' upon it. While it can be useful to have physical 'weapons' for use in ritual, it is also instructive to understand their operation in other spheres. For example, my desire to write, and the decision to write about sorcery, is the operation of the wand. The use of language to order and analyse my thoughts; the act of writing itself is the dagger. The computer screen upon which my words appear to me, prompting new ideas and associations even as I write, is the chalice, and the resulting printout, which manifests the whole, is the pentacle. The lamp in this case, is any form of illuminatory technique which I use to aid the free-flow of creativity.

Like any game, sorcery relies more on the qualities and skill of the player, rather than the physical surroundings or the equipment being used. Similarly, both games and magic have an absurd quality about them. You may find it incredible that other people seem to invest so much importance in the outcome of a football game, yet have no problem yourself believing that scratching planetary symbols onto a candle will bring about a change in the world. Alternatively, you might vociferously champion your own team and wonder what the fuss is about when batty occultists argue over who has the 'authentic magical tradition.' But both sorcery and games require practice, suspension of disbelief, and gnosis, that cessation of the internal dialogue which may last from a few seconds to several hours.

RESPONSIVE SORCERY

To be effective, your approach to sorcery needs to be responsive to changes in your life situation. It can best be understood as not so much an approach to getting a "free lunch" out of the universe, but as an approach to maximising your effectiveness within different spheres of action. For example, there is little point in enchanting for a new job, if you lack confidence to the extent that you are going to blow each interview that you work for. It is often said that magic seems to work through the easiest route possible, and this should be borne in mind. Finally in this introduction to sorcery, I want to look at some popular areas for sorcery intervention.

Protection

Protection spells are popular, but what exactly does 'protection' mean? Protection from earthquakes, mugging, meteor strikes, or what? Does then protection mean safety? All questions of safety are relative. Why is it that you desire protection? Is it that you are clumsy, or that you don't look where you are going? If this is the case, use techniques which drag your attention to what's around you at any one moment. Cultivate the danger/alert sense I discussed in Chapter Three. There is also the issue of "protection" against magical attack, to which some people become concerned with to an obsessive degree. Well don't worry about it, because there isn't any. Ninety-nine percent of 'magical attack' is self-inflicted, and, no effective magician (with an eye to his street-cred) will ever admit to being 'magically attacked' and not doing something about it—at the time. Usually, people who go on about magical attack are covering up some glaring inadequacy within themselves, and also suffering from an over-inflated sense of importance. Again, having a finely-tuned 'warning sense' is of more use here, as is being able to keep one's feet on the ground, as it were.

Love, And Getting Laid Magic

Finding a partner, soul-mate or one-night stand via magical means is extremely popular, and the ability to bring lovers together or cause them to fly apart, as part of the sorcerer's repertoire of powers, goes some way to explaining how both can be subjects of respect and fear simultaneously. There are many shades of Love Magic. At a basic level, it does help if you are observant, have skills in reading all the subtle signs of non-verbal communication, and know when to speak, and when to keep silent. Love Magic is very much about working with other people. It is also important to be able to clearly distinguish between a sexual impulse and a relationship—that is, are you enchanting to make a link between yourself and the target person, from the basis of a quick knee-trembler or the possibility of a long-term relationship. It's surprising how many people confuse the two. It should be recognised that often, our 'desires' about what constitutes an ideal lover are usually contextual, and very often, differ from our actual needs. In my experience, casting Love Magic spells with a particular person in mind never works out satisfactorily. I have personally found it more effective to enchant for "the lover I need" rather than "the lover I want." I do find it slightly odd that, in Western approaches to magic, Love Spells are thought to be fairly innocuous, while cursing magic is generally held to reprehensible. Has no one ever thought how much of a curse becoming involved with another person can be? If you are ever tempted to interfere in the drama of someone else's relationship troubles, do bear this in mind—before you wade in, wand blazing to magically influence the relationship, think how *you* would feel if you found that someone had done the same with you? Although you can influence people into dropping their trousers/knickers for you, it is generally more effective in the long-term to work on your own powers of seduction and attraction. Sex is magical, and can be made more so, but if you are a short, spotty herbert with the charisma of a brick, then all the spells in the world are not going to make *Playboy* models fawn at your feet—unless you perhaps enchant for wealth and have major plastic surgery, or discover some other quality or aspect which you can enhance towards this eventual goal. By which time, like as not, sex will not seem quite so much an imperative as it once did. Issues of Love and Sex are particularly important for magicians as, in dealing with them, at some point we have to acknowledge the presence and complexity of other people.

Healing

Healing is again, a difficult area. It is an area that demands results, and approaches to magical healing tend to become fairly methodical and common-sense. It is interesting to note that such down-to-earth techniques and methodologies tend to have been squeezed out from the main body of Western Occultism, into areas such as Witchcraft or Spiritualism, where participants are not afraid to come down off the astral plane and do something practical. Despite the gross industry in new-age spawned healers, the use of magical techniques in healing is an area which requires much work and investigation. If you are interested in this area, forget past-life regressions, diagnosing auras, chakra massage and all the other exotic stuff, and just go for a simple 'client gets better' result. There is an example of a Servitor for healing in the next chapter and it's worth bearing in mind that, if you become an accomplished healer, then people do sit up and take notice. Developing a 'Healer Persona' can be useful, both for projecting a certain ambiance and for maintaining a 'professional distance' between yourself and your clients (see Ego Magic). The desire to be a healer must also be rigorously analysed from time to time. The desire to heal can become obsessive to the point where you are more interested in preserving your self-image as a healer than the actual needs of your clients.

Cursing

Offensive or aggressive magic is one of those areas which, while controversial, nonetheless, requires looking at. A common reaction to cursing is to say that it is wrong, unethical, or incurs karmic consequences. These arguments neatly ignore the fact that curse-magic is of a most ancient lineage, and often appears, in its most sophisticated forms, in tribal and shamanic societies. Historically, curses are thrown when recourse to other forms of retaliation are not possible—if standing up to being oppressed gets you a rifle-butt in the face, then magical action might well be the only option left. It's difficult to talk about ethics and karma with someone who keeps kicking you. Again, magic is about taking responsibility for your actions, so if you do have to curse someone, be aware that (a) it is the most appropriate course of action (b) you can handle any consequences, and (c) you get the result you want. Remember that life situations are always going to be much more complex than any white magic/black magic dichotomies, hence the chaos emphasis on developing your own guidelines. Is it a curse if you cause a multiple-rapist to become increasingly clumsy in his activities, so that eventually he is exposed and identified? Is it unethical to perform a Requiem Mass in absentia for a friend with terminal cancer who has clearly expressed to you his wish to die?

Twin Glamours—Wealth And Fame

Wealth tends to be a condition which one aspires to, or a condition which has been (to varying degrees), attained. Thus one may look at one's life and say "I have wealth" or "I wish I was wealthy." Before we go much further, the question of 'What do we mean by wealth?' should be dealt with. Dictionary definitions of Wealth go along the lines of 'abundance of material resources.' However, money is only one aspect of Wealth Magic. It is not merely about accumulating money and consumer goods. Desires can be deceptive. Before looking at the desire for Wealth, let's take a look at some other manifestations of desire. Sex is a good place to start. There is a tendency to behave as though sexual desire is simple—a knee-jerk stimulus- "Phwoarr!"-response which sets the heart a-pounding and hormones racing around. Desire falls upon us, immediately and physically—it can be anything from a wistful glance in someone's direction to a palpable shock which leaves you gasping for breath. Yet, as we all, in our introspective moments know, sexual desire is very complex, very powerful, and subject to change when least expect it—just when we think we are safe. A 'gay' man suddenly finds himself wanting a woman. A 'straight' man realises, to his horror, that he finds himself unable to take his eyes off the boy next door. Sexual desire can be dangerous, and much depends on how the ego survives such transitions. Fame is another good one to examine. Particularly so for me, as, without appearing prideful, I know that I have, over the years, attained a degree of acclaim, a certain reputation, and, albeit within a small subculture, a degree of recognition. Now fame has much in common with Wealth. It is something which you have either attained, or you aspire to—in the sense of thinking "Look at so-and-so, I wish *I* was famous." Now, although it is entirely possible that, somewhere, back in the days of my neophyte-hood, I may have performed an enchantment to bring fame. But, as far as I know, I did at no time say to myself 'by doing this I will become famous', or, 'I want to become a *name* on the Occult Scene. It might sound ingenuous, but I did not realise, for a long time, that I was beginning to gain a reputation of sorts. What did I do? Firstly, I began to write. I began to write because I wanted to get occult magazines, and could not afford the subscription fee. I was encouraged to write. All occult magazine editors are on the lookout for new writers. My High Priestess encouraged me to write. I found that writing was an excellent way of ordering my thoughts. I began to enjoy writing. After all, who doesn't get a thrill from seeing their name in a magazine? It is even more satisfying to receive payment for writing.

Secondly, I began to speak in public. The reasons why I did this are more complex. I was crap at presenting myself to people, and, as I was doing a course which necessitated that I present myself to people, I deliberately put myself in a position where I had to present myself to an audience. I became the student representative for my Course, which meant that I had to deal with the Student Union Council, the lecturers, and the Academic Board. Slowly, I began to adjust to these demands, and even more slowly, I began to enjoy it. From lectures, I jumped to doing courses and workshops, and finally began to appreciate the skills and techniques that I had been trained to utilise, albeit in a different setting. When you begin to raise your profile into the public domain, you attract attention. I was genuinely shocked when someone said to me "well you do have a reputation for being such-and-such." I was dismayed and angered when details of my private life became a matter of comment in certain magazines. At times, I would enjoy hearing rumours and strangers' opinions of me from another source, but for a long time, I resisted, even hated the suggestion that I was becoming a public figure on the small, incestuous occult scene. But also, I was learning some important lessons, which I will come onto shortly. The problem I have with the idea of Wealth Magic is that it is too nebulous, too much of a long-term vision. Sexual desire is physical and immediate. But wealth and fame have a lot in common. I look into the window of a computer store at the latest models and wish I had the money to buy one, without having to save or do overtime. Similarly, I have looked with envy upon someone who is apparently popular, easy in company, and appears to attract the girls/boys whom I dare not speak to. Wealth and fame are glamours. They are desires which have power over us because we feel that we *lack* something. They remind us that we are not *at ease* with our present circumstances. Much has been written about the relationship between Wealth Magic and Jupiter, to which is attributed the quality of expansiveness. Yet it is impossible to be expansive if you feel at odds with yourself. Before you can become expansive, you have to have worked with the Solar quality of Confidence. I have found that a useful way to approach Confidence is to identify it as a skill—the skill of being *relaxed in the immediate present.* Relaxation, of course, is essential if you are going to present yourself to people. It is also the unacknowledged key to magical success. If you are relaxed, then you have freed yourself from the patterns of your past, and ceased to project desires in the imminent future. If you are relaxed, then you see any situation as it is, not how it 'ought' or 'should' be. Yet even this is not enough. Confidence requires a degree of Self-Love, which in turn requires self-awareness, particularly of your own nested desire-complexes. Surface desires are often blinds thrown up by the Ego, to disguise something which cannot be admitted into awareness. Such conflicts eventually become the magician's nemesis. A man might sublimate his desire for young flesh by becoming a scoutmaster, priest or youth worker, but how long will the facade hold up? From the Self-Love of Solar magic we jump to the dynamics of Love magic. Until you accept yourself, you will never be able to accept other people as independent beings, and so you will be continually disappointed when other people fail to act in the way that they 'ought' to. To be expansive to others, you have to learn how to interact with other people successfully. You have to be *attentive* to others, and aware, of course, of how they *see* you. What else is required? Mars, the magic of energy, drive, determination, discipline, cool-headedness. The poise of a sniper waiting for the right moment to fire. Also Thought Magic, the way of planning, strategy, of being able to examine a situation and working out Plan A, Plan B, what I will do if things go awry; the ability to look at resources, whether they be material, skills, or contacts. And then there is Death Magic. I have a plan. It is exciting. I can see how it could go very well. But, after all the planning has been done, it looks more unfeasible. Do I go ahead anyway? Or have I the strength to kill it and do something else? Death Magic is also the magic of boundaries, of self-imposed limitations. Not forgetting Sexual Magic. In Qabalah, Sexuality is attributed to the sphere of Yesod, which is also the sphere of seduction, glamour, and illusion. Sex reminds us of our vulnerability, and we can all too easily become caught up in the desire for fast clothes, big cars, attractive partners and four-poster beds. But if you need these things to feel sexy, then it's just possible that something is going wrong. The roots of feeling attractive lie in Self-Love, and we're back to Ego Magic again.

If you desire Wealth, don't dwell on it. There is an old axiom that if you are bound by something, you will never attain it. The Unconscious (what Spare called "the greatest magician") does not understand this concept. Each time you desire wealth, you are reminding yourself of things which you *lack*. Similarly, those who go around declaring that they want to be famous will end up being a prat. Which is not the kind of fame which is going to do you any good. Work in the other spheres of magic. If you are involved in a business or enterprise, do Business Magic, which is merely the application of the other rays into your work—learning about people, learning how to lead, how to manage, how to inspire, how to effect your will. Learn how to have doors 'open' for you. Learn how to speak to the right people at the right time. Learn the subtle arts of Impression Management.

A useful archetype in this respect is the Emperor, Prince or Mandarin. Read Machiavelli, for a start, and then examine the histories of great imperial figures. How does one act towards an emperor? With reverence, for insolence is courting death. An emperor likes flattery, but not obsequiousness. An emperor has great power, but is also aware of the responsibility which that power brings. Emperors are famed for their expansiveness. They must give the best gifts, as their reputation is at stake. A successful emperor knows how to make use of his resources, and knows how to generate respect in others. And respect is important. It is the basis of trust. Trust is not immediate. It must be earnt. How must you act to win the respect of others? Find out, and do it.

Wealth is something which you either look forwards to, or have attained. In the Indian tradition, it is, like wisdom, a siddha, which is to say an achievement—something which happens gradually. On the Tantric path, all so-called magical powers are merely by-products of one's passage through the world. Other people may well attribute those things to the magician before he himself realises it. Ganesha is a useful deity. He brings wealth, but he is not attached to it or weighed down by the necessity of it, he is relaxed in the world. So how can we obtain a useful definition of Wealth Magic? I would say that Wealth Magic is the process of learning to recognise and enjoy one's immediate circumstances. Expansiveness is characterised as "high spirits, generosity and willingness to talk," all of which implies a sense of relaxation in the immediate present.

THE EMPTY-HANDED GESTURE

The mark of an advanced sorcerer is the use of the so-called 'Empty-Handed Gesture', which is acts of sorcery without use of any physical props or formalised settings. Practice in visualisation, a quiet confidence which falls just short of being arrogance, and the ability to free an established desire from the ties of the ego-complex are requisite skills, all of which are developed through more formal sorcery practice. The advanced sorcerer may only use a series of gestures, and rely on visualisation and make-believe to create the space he requires for magical action. A 'successful' sorcerer need not be surrounded by icons of material wealth, but all the same, tends to appear to be "lucky", or seemingly have a facility for being "in the right place at the right time." The effective sorcerer pays attention to what happens in his life, noting the hidden patterns that run through the apparent chaos of everyday life, and acknowledging the intrusion of fortuitous coincidence into his life. While he may claim a high success rate, the chances are that he is selective about what he chooses to enchant for.

CHAPTER SIX

CHAOS SERVITORS

EVOCATION

The term evocation means 'to call forth' and it is used to describe all magical techniques which serve to bring forth some kind of entity into a defined space, such as a bottle or a crystal, or simply a visualised form which has shape and character. The practice of evocation has generally come to be associated with the so-called 'demons' of Grimoires such as *The Keys of Solomon*, and has, in some quarters, acquired a dubious reputation. When you evoke a spirit, it is usually to get it to perform some kind of 'task' for you. Again, such pragmatism is seen as 'unspiritual' and therefore an act of 'lesser magic'. In other quarters, evocation is similarly frowned on, as it is felt that magicians should not 'order' spirits about. Neither arguments are convincing, and evocation is a very useful magical technique which, once the basic elements have been grasped, has numerous applications.

A Servitor is an entity consciously created or generated, using evocatory techniques, to perform a task or service. In the Western Esoteric Tradition, such entities are sometimes referred to as 'Thought-Forms', while in Tibetan magic, for example, they are known as 'Tulpas'.

Servitors can be usefully deployed to perform a wide range of tasks or functions on your behalf.

SERVITOR DESIGN SEQUENCE

The following gives a basic approach to designing Servitors for a wide range of tasks, and demonstrates how you can utilise some of the techniques presented earlier. In this sequence, Servitors are treated very much in cybernetic terms, as though they are some kind of programmable astral-machine.

1. Define General Intent

The first step in designing a Servitor is to decide the general sphere of influence into which your intention falls, such as healing, protection, binding, harmony, luck, divination, mood enhancement, success in..., and so forth. Defining your general intent will assist you if you wish to use symbols and magical correspondences in creating your Servitor. For example, if you were interested in creating a Servitor to act within the sphere of Healing, then you could assemble any associations, symbols, emotions, memories, etc. which you relate to the concept of Healing. By consulting a book of magical correspondences such as '777', you could build up chains of correspondences— planetary figures, scents, colours, planetary hours etc. How far you go in this direction is very much a matter of personal choice.

2. Defining Specific Intent

Here, you are creating the core of the Servitor's purpose—the Statement of Intent which is analogous to the Servitor's aetheric DNA. Formulating the Servitor's Statement of Intent may necessitate a good deal of self-analysis into your motivations, desires, realistic projections of goals, etc. As in all sorcery operations, it is appropriate to use techniques such as SWOT outlined in Chapter Five, or ask advice from your preferred form of divination. To continue the example of a Healing Servitor, an appropriate Statement of Intent might be "To promote rapid recovery and health in...(name)..."

Once you have determined the appropriate Intent to form the basis of your Servitor, the Statement can be rendered into a sigil, as explained in the previous chapter.

This example shows how the Statement of Intent was turned into a sigil, which, during the 'Launch' of the Servitor, will become part of its form.

3. Symbols Appropriate To The Servitor's Task

There is a wealth of magical and mythic symbols which you can draw upon when creating a Servitor, which can be used to represent different qualities, abilities and attributes. And there is the symbolism of colour, smell, sound and other senses to draw upon. To refine the 'program' which forms the basis for your Servitor, you could embellish the sigil by adding other symbols.

This illustration develops the Healing Servitor. Its core sigil has been placed within a hexagram, and the number 7 has been added to it. Here, the hexagram represents balance, health, life enhancement and Solar qualities, and forms the elemental symbols of Fire (representing healing fire, the burning up of fever) and Water (representing expulsion of toxins through sweat, calming influences). The number 7 represents the idea of harmony, and also represents the duration of the Servitor's operation. The entire figure forms the 'instructions' for the Servitor which will be visualised as forming a part of it, during its launch phase.

Symbols: The Language Of The Deep Mind

To get to grips with how symbols work, perhaps the best analogy is of the Deep (unconscious) Mind of being like an ocean which is dotted with "islands"—each island being an individual self. This analogy emphasises how individuals, events and images are connected at a deep level, in contrast to the prevailing psychological models of mind, which tend to emphasise the division of the psyche into subjective and objective, inner and outer, mind and body. To extend this analogy further, the island of selfhood from which arises our sense of being unique individuals; of "I-ness" can be likened to an iceberg. Most of the mass of which, is below the surface—that is, below self-awareness. This iceberg arises from the Deep Mind and is in continual interaction with it. Both iceberg and ocean are comple-mentary expressions of consciousness. The iceberg is a mass of psychic structures which form from the internalisation of experience into thoughts, feelings, memories, attitudes and beliefs. There are those which we regard as uniquely Personal, those structures which are formed through the process of education and enculturation, which are Social, and those archetypal images which are of a Mythic nature. The term embedded is used to refer to the mass of psychic structures that form the basis of our world-view, yet are below the surface of the Deep Mind. This world view is a product of our culture, but it also has inbuilt contradictions which depend from the Mythic world. For example, we tend to believe that Magic is impossible or supernatural, yet the Myths that society tells itself, through books, films and stories gives us, at least temporarily, the "hope" that this is not the case. The iceberg of individuality arises from the medium of mind which we all share.

The iceberg itself can be seen as a complex lattice, composed of the interconnected psychic structures, from which arises the sense of personality, and our sense of unique "I-ness". These icebergs are not immutable or static entities (though we tend to regard ourselves as such). They are continually being shaped by experience. One might even say that Magic, as a way of inducing change and transformation, works by heating up the iceberg from within, so that the individual becomes more responsive and adaptive to the tides of consciousness that flow around the psyche, rather than remaining frozen and rigid! Experiences that remain close to the "surface" of waking awareness are organised using the faculty of language, the main resource by which we communicate experiences to each other, and order experience to ourselves. However, the deeper that an experience becomes embedded below the surface—into the Deep Mind, the more likely it is to become encoded as a symbol.

We react far more quickly to symbols than we do to written information; very simple graphic symbols can convey a great deal of information that would take up much more space if written out. Road signs are a good example of the immediacy of symbols—imagine the chaos that would ensue if road signs were all composed of words! Symbols are defined as non-linguistic graphic figures, which represent a more abstract quality, idea, principle or concept. In terms of the iceberg analogy they are encapsulations of experiences, which "contain", bound into their structure, emotions, memories, and other associations. All of which can be "freed" when the symbol is focused upon. Symbols play an important role in Magic, as they are the common "language" which is shared by both the Waking Awareness and the Deep Mind. Magical systems are bodies of technique and frameworks for ordering experience, with recourse to specific sets of symbols, which gradually becomes embedded in the Deep Mind. Magical exercises, for example, meditation on Tarot card images, serve to "fix" symbols in our minds, and the Deep Mind often clothes itself in those symbols to communicate insights and information to the waking mind. Some magical symbols, such as the pentagram and hexagram, for example, appear in many different cultures. It does appear that some symbols are "universal", in that the understanding of them is not limited to cultural barriers.

The power of symbols is that they give access to strata of the Deep Mind with an immediacy and intensity that written or spoken language cannot. They bring into awareness vast amounts of information which may be too abstract or complex to process semantically. They can also be used to tap memories of experience that has very powerful emotional associations, which are brought into awareness when the symbol is focused on. Although symbols are usually thought of as graphic designs, there are other "carriers" of information which can be thought of as types of symbol. These symbols are media which have a very powerful effect on us (although we are not always aware of it) and carry associations which are brought into awareness (or at least stirred) when we encounter them. Such media have a very important role in Magical practice, and examples are: Sound, Smell and Colour.

Graphic Symbols

The design of Graphic symbols in Magic is very much part of the glamour and mystery the occult has for many people—books full of weird symbols and figures which are purported to have all kinds of mysterious, inherent powers, and geometric figures chalked on the floor to summon Demons. Examples of Graphic figures can be found in many magical textbooks, and fall into three categories:

i) Those which derive from magical or religious systems
ii) Those constructed by the magician for a specific purpose.
iii) Figures which arise from the Deep Mind.

The first category includes the type of figures referred to above, examples of which include astrological and planetary symbols, geometric patterns such as the pentagram, and "secret" alphabets. It is generally held that personally designed (i.e., Sigils) or, as in the third case, "discovered" symbols are more beneficial than using someone else's symbols, as the former will have more personal associations and reflect the users psycho-cosm more accurately than anything from a book. If you are already assimilating magical symbol systems however, there is no reason why you shouldn't incorporate them into Servitor design. Again, this comes down to personal preference.

4. Is There A Time Factor To Consider?

Here, you should consider the duration of the Servitor's operation. In other words, do you want the Servitor to be 'working' continuously, or only at specific periods? Here, you may wish to take into account phases of the moon, astrological conjunctions or planetary hours, for example, which could be added into the Servitor's symbolic instructions. The Healing Servitor above for example, was instructed to be active for a period of seven days, affecting its target recipient for seven minutes, at seven hour intervals. This instruction serves to reinforce the number symbolism and association with harmony. It is also at this point that you should consider what happens after the Servitor has performed its task. Generally, there are two forms of Servitor; those which are task-specific, and those which have a general-purpose nature. For the moment though, I'll concentrate on task-specific Servitors. These are Servitors which are created for a specific task, such as the example of the Healing Servitor created to work on a particular person. It is generally held to be preferable that when a Servitor has completed its task, the Servitor should be disassembled by its creator. There are two approaches to doing this. Firstly, one can encode a "self-destruct" instruction into the Servitor at the time of its creation, where the duration of its existence is defined in terms of the duration of its task or the fulfillment of a specific condition. For example, the Healing Servitor could be defined so that it's sigilised Statement of Intent is: "To promote rapid recovery and health in...(name)...working at 7/7/7 intervals, the sum of which is the spell of your life."

Another approach is to perform a ritual 'reabsorption' of the Servitor, mentally drawing it back from its task, taking it apart by visualization, taking back the original desire which sparked its creation, and taking apart or destroying any material base which you have created for it. While classical occult theory says that if you do not look after your thought-forms, they will wander around the astral plane annoying people, there is good psychological sense for terminating the 'life' of Servitors which have completed their assigned task—that you are reclaiming responsibility for that desire-complex which you used to create the Servitor.

5. Is A Name Required?

The Servitor can be given a name which can be used, in addition to its sigil, for creating, powering, or controlling it. A name also acts to further create a Servitor's persona. A name can reflect the Servitor's task, or be formed from a mantric sigil of its Statement of Intent. The example Healing Servitor was given the name TUMMYHUM, a rather whimsical reference to its function.

6. Is A Material Base Required?

The Material base is some physical focus for the Servitor's existence. This can help to define the Servitor as an individual entity, and can be used if you need to recall the Servitor for any reason. Examples of a material base include bottles, rings, crystals, small figurines as used in fantasy role-playing or figures crafted from modeling compounds. Bodily fluids can be applied to the material base to increase the perceived link between creator and entity. This is very much a matter of personal taste. Alternatively, the Servitor can remain freely mobile as an aetheric entity. I tend to find that one-shot, task-specific Servitors can be left as aetheric entities, while for entities which have more of along-term use, a material base is often helpful. For others, it might be possible to link their use to a specific, identifiable, state of consciousness, which forms part of the core associations which one builds up for a Servitor.

It is also possible to link a Servitor to a specific smell, such as a perfume or essential oil, so that each time the oil is applied, the Servitor is activated. This can be particularly useful when creating Servitors for general Healing, Protection, or enhancement of a particular mood. A dab of the perfume can be put onto the Servitor's material base, and the perfume should be inhaled during the launch of the entity.

7. Is A Specific Shape Required?

Servitors can be created to have any desired shape, from tiny homunculi to morphic spheres capable of extruding any required appendage. The shape you choose to identify with this particular thought-form can add another level of representational identity to the entity. A common practice though, is to visualise the Servitor as a featureless sphere, pulsing with energy, glowing with appro-priately chosen colours, into which has been impressed, its sigilised instructions.

SERVITOR LAUNCH SEQUENCE

Once you have designed a Servitor, the next step is to 'Launch' upon its appointed mission. There are many different ways of doing this, and you can experiment with the techniques described earlier in this book. The following sequence can be experimented with as an introductory example to Servitor Work.

LAUNCH PROCEDURE

1. Banishing
2. Statement of Intent
3. Lightning Flash Exercise
4. Airburst Servitor Launch
5. Banishing Reprise

Banishing Ritual

Begin facing east and stand, with your arms by your sides, head tilted slightly upwards, breathing slowly and deeply. Clear your mind of thoughts.

1. Inhale, and reach upwards with your right hand, visualising a point of light just beyond your fingertips.

2. Bring your hand slowly down the centreline of your body, to point between your feet. Exhale, and visualise a beam of white light passing down your body, from above your head to below your feet.

3. Inhale, and stretch out your arms so that they form a Tau-cross. Exhale, and visualise a beam of white light running across your body, from left to right.

4. Inhale, and fold your arms across your chest. Exhale, and as you do so, visualise a blaze of light spreading across your body, expanding from the two axis previously formed. Breathe in and out deeply, feeling yourself to be charged with energy. This completes the first stage of the banishing and is generally known as the Cross of Light.

5. Next, inhale, and trace a pentagram in the air before you, beginning at the apex, drawing down to the lower left-hand point, then across to the right, across to the left, down to the lower right point, and back to the apex. Exhale, vibrating the letters **I A O** (EEE-AH-OH), visualising the pentagram glowing brightly with white light.

6. Repeat this for the South, West, and North cardinal points.

7. Then raise your arms and declare the litany:

About me flare five-pointed stars
Above my head the infinite stars
Every Man and Every Woman is a star,
Behold, a circle of Stars."

Statement Of Intent

Now that you have centered yourself within the ritual space, you can make the Statement of intent, for example: "It is my will to evoke a Servitor for...(mission)..."

Lightning Flash Exercise

This exercise is used for 'energising' oneself. It combines, breathing, visualisation, bodily awareness and the build-up and subsequent discharge of tension. It is loosely based on the Middle Pillar exercise used in Western Qabalah.

1. Stand, feet apart, arms reaching upwards, eyes closed, head tilted slightly upwards.

2. Visualize yourself as an oak tree, standing alone in a bleak and desolate landscape. It is night, and the stars are above you. Be aware of your breathing, deep and slow; that you stand firm, rooted in the earth, yet reaching for the sky.

3. Around you, a storm begins to build. Let your breathing quicken. A wind whips up around you, beginning to shake your firmness. Electrical tension grows, and you can feel a distant throbbing in the earth.

4. Let these sensations build to a fever pitch; your breathing becomes faster and shallower. Let yourself rock forwards slightly on your feet, so that you are straining upwards but feeling yourself shake with growing tension.

5. When you can stand this no more, there is a deafening crack, and a bolt of lightning shoots downwards from the heavens. It strikes you, causing you to shudder violently. You feel the tremendous energy of the lightning bolt course through you, passing down through your roots and into the depths of the earth.

6. From the deep earth there comes an answering tremor of force. A pulse of energy surges upwards, flashing up your body and carrying your consciousness upwards into the sky until you become, for a brief moment, a star shining in infinite space.

7. Let your arms come slowly down to the sides of your body. Bring your feet together, and place the first two fingers of your right hand to your lips. Feel yourself to be calm, yet super-charged with energy.

Airburst Servitor Launching

This is a simple exercise which can be used for launching Servitors and enchantments. It can easily be adapted for group use, and is based on the idea of 'Raising the Power-Cone' in modern Wicca.

1. Begin, seated in a comfortable posture—the Dragon Asana is ideal. Breathe slowly and easily.

2. Feel your body to be charged with energy, and let this energy coalesce into a sphere of white light, in the region of your solar plexus, as you breathe in and out.

3. As you breathe, visualise a cord of light extruding from your solar plexus, until it is at least two feet in front of you.

4. And now the cord begins to grow upwards, forming a column of pulsing power, rising towards the ceiling (assuming you are doing this indoors). When you feel confident in your visualization, let the column of energy become free-standing, so that it is no longer attached to you. This sphere is the raw mass from which you will form your Servitor.

5. Now focus your awareness at the top of the column. It begins to bulge as you concentrate upon it, forming an enlarging sphere which, as it grows, draws the rest of the column upwards.

6. Once the sphere is formed, you can begin to 'programme' the Servitor by forming the sphere into a shape (if you have chosen one) or visualising the Servitor's instruction symbols merging into it. If you are using a name for the Servitor, this can be chanted as a mantra, with each utterance feeding power into the Servitor. It can also be visualised as flashing with any chosen colour sequence. When visualising the Servitor forming, it can be useful sometimes to visualise the core sigil/symbols which make up the Servitor's instruction code as a strand of DNA, which develops into cells, musculature, or a nervous system. Alternatively, you could visualise the Servitor's form building up from chains of sigils, in appropriate colours.

7. As you do this, let your breathing become faster and more intense. Feel that you are moving towards some kind of climax. Begin a mental or vocal countdown from 10 to 1...with each number, the feeling of tension intensifies, the Servitor begins to pulse as though it has a heartbeat—your visualisations, chanting, etc. becomes more frenzied. As you reach 1...take a deep breath and shout "BLAST OFF!"—visualise the Servitor shooting forth into space at high speed, and let yourself collapse.

8. Let yourself relax for a moment. If you feel it is necessary, repeat the Banishing ritual which you used at the beginning of the rite.

GENERAL-PURPOSE SERVITORS

The example given earlier is that of a task-specific Servitor; that is, one specifically created to perform a task relating to one particular individual. However, a Servitor could be created which had a general provenance of Healing, which was not targeted at one person. There are a number of advantages to using more generalised Servitors. Firstly, they can be regarded as 'expert' systems which learn from being given a task to execute—as if the more healing tasks you give a Servitor, the better it seems to become at healing.

Secondly, continued use of the Servitor, with successful results, builds up "confidence" in its activity on the part of those who use it. With a more generalised Servitor, anyone who knows its activation sequence (such as a mantra, sigil, or visualisation sequence) can employ it to work at a given task. One example of this form of Servitor is the entity ICANDOO. ICANDOO ("I-can-do") was created at an open group workshop in Servitor creation. The name of the Servitor was also its mantra for summoning it, and its general brief was to assist those who used it for overcoming any obstacles that crossed them. ICANDOO was created by a group of twelve people, and all of them used the Servitor throughout the day, to assist them with problems of one sort or another. In the design sequence, the Servitor was given the ability to divide itself holographically, so that each segment contained the powers and abilities of the original entity. On a still further level of generalisation, you can create Servitors who have no specific function or provenance, saving that they serve to increase the success of one's own magics. Such Servitors can be used in both major and minor acts of magic, and are particularly useful in acts of enchantment, divination, or illumination. An example of such a Servitor is GoHu, which was given the appearance of a black, slightly concave, mirror. Activated by visualisation and mantra, GoHu was used as a receptacle into which were projected sigilised desires and other enchantments. By changing the angle of orientation to its surface, it could be visualised as though it were a bowl, out of which ideas and images floated, and I often mentally activated it prior to using divinatory systems.

SERVITOR DEPENDENCY

It is generally held that each usage of a Servitor serves to 'feed' it, and that each result which is rated as a success, serves to enhance its power. It is also a good idea to get into the habit of attributing any occurrences within the sphere of activity of that Servitor, to its work. This can lead to problems, though. In 1992 I created a Servitor called "Eureka." Its given sphere of activity was that of Illumination—inspiration, new ideas, the boosting of creativity and brainstorming in general. Initially, the Servitor exceeded all my expectations of its performance. I used it to stimulate new ideas for writing, lecturing and facilitating seminars and workshops. With a colleague, it became a focus for brainstorming—acting as a Third Mind arising from conversation. Each time we made a creative leap, or an idea formed became something workable in practice, the power of the Servitor was boosted. In 1993, the activity of Eureka was linked with the Neptune-Uranus conjunction with the result that, on April 22nd, as Neptune and Uranus began to retrograde, Eureka went "off-line." The immediate result of this was that I suddenly found it much harder to get into a flow of creative thinking. It seemed that Eureka had become such a dominant element in the dynamics of my own creative process that, once it was removed, I found it much harder to get into the appropriate frame of mind. I had become dependent upon the Servitor. Eventually, the Servitor was recalled and disassembled in such a way that a 'splinter' of its original power survived as a focus for illumination. Having been made wiser by this experience, I only occasionally use this fragment of the original Servitor as a focus for creativity.

VIRAL SERVITORS

It is possible to instruct Servitors to replicate or reproduce themselves. Approaches to this include instructing the Servitor to replicate itself as a form of cell-division, following cybernetic or viral parameters, or to create a Servitor which 'gives birth' according to particular parameters, such as time-units, astrological transits, or when the target of the Servitor carries out a particular behavior. An early test of this concept was that of a Servitor despatched to assist in the recovery of property withheld from its owner. Once a set deadline had been passed, the Servitor began to generate a field of 'confusion'—lost keys, electrical blowouts and other minor but annoying problems. After a second deadline the Servitor replicated itself so that the confusion field intensified. As soon as the recipient of the Servitor returned the property, the Servitors ceased to function. Evidence of the Servitors' actions—the intensification of minor problems into strange poltergeist-type phenomenon—was gathered by talking to associates of the target. Viral Servitors are particularly appropriate for long-term enchantments, such as increasing the probability of one's magic being successful, or in healing and general protection workings.

CHAO-MINES

Chao-Mines are not, strictly speaking, Servitors, but are formed using the same techniques. They can be considered as localised aetheric storage and transmission units for Chaos energy. They are generally visualised as spheroids with eight arrows or antennae radiating from them, which flash randomly with all possible colours. Chao-Mines are created to manipulate probability in favour of fortuitous occurrences, bizarre synchronicities, and the generally weird and wonderful. They are usually created at places which are habitually used for magical activity, or which generally have an association of 'good vibes' and pleasant happenings.

SERVITOR PROGRAMMING LANGUAGES

The use of Servitors within a quasi-cybernetics paradigm was originally only semi-serious, as I wrote a brief "User's Guide" to working with Servitors, in the style of a Computer Manual. Over time however, approaching Servitors from the perspective of Information Technology did generate some interesting ideas for developing their use. One of these ideas is the analogy already made between the sigilised Statement of Intent which is the core of the Servitor—its *raison d'être*, if you like—and computer code—the instructions which it carries out. This analogy has been developed in two ways. The first was to develop the code into sigil-circuits, an example of which is given below. Here are the Servitor's basic instructions:

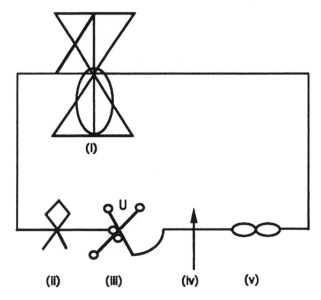

(i)

(II)   (III)   (Iv)   (v)

(i) has been enhanced using the rune Othel (ii) the Kamea of Mars (iii) and the rune Tir (iv). The infinity symbol (v) keeps the sequence looping. The mixing of symbols from different systems does not seem to make any difference—you use the symbols that you find appropriate, and obviously the option is there to create your own sigil-circuit elements.

Another development, related to the above, was to look at Servitor action (and later, enchantment in general) in terms of flowcharts. Computer program flowcharts contain options such as "IF...THEN..." If x = 1, then y = "print screen"—If y doesn't equal 1, then no action is taken. A Servitor can be given an IF...THEN option. For example, if a particular condition is fulfilled, then the Servitor becomes active. Developing this idea led to the creation of extremely detailed flowcharts, with 'controller' Servitors commanding subroutines and subprograms formed from Servitors given specific tasks within an overall program.

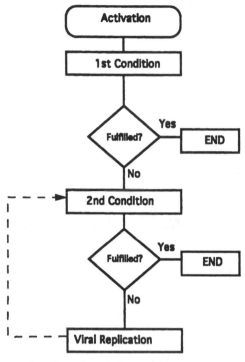

This sample flowchart shows the operation of the viral Servitor discussed above. This idea in itself gives rise to some basic considerations of how we approach Sorcery operations in general. The general approach to 'results magic' is to locate one point in an unfolding situation and 'nudge' it (gently or not) until a result which is more or less in accordance with your stated desire manifests. Some operations may be fairly specific in their scope, while others may be of a long-term nature, but generally speaking, it is of a "one-shot" nature. Once you start to look at situations from the perspective of a program or flowchart, you have the possibility of taking into account a diverse number of elements which have a bearing on that situation.

FUNCTIONAL SPIRITS

Another approach to Evocation is working with Spirits which have a provenance over a particular situation or experience. Entities such as these are detailed in Grimoires such as *The*

Lesser Key of Solomon the King, which are handbooks of spirits, giving details of spirits' typical forms, names, sigils, and how to conjure them. The spirits in books such as the Lesser Key have bizarre names, even more bizarre appearances, yet their powers are directly functional and useful. For example, RAUM appears as a blackbird, and can create love, reconcile enemies, or destroy cities and reputations.

The standard approach to summoning these spirits is to use the time-honoured magical ritual, wherein the entities are called forth into a triangle, and ceremonially bound to the magician's will. However, there is also another possibility, which is simply that of summoning a Spirit when you find yourself in an appropriate situation. The following example illustrates this process.

All of us, at one time or another, suffer from being stuck in traffic, from freeway jams to slow-moving queues of people. Wouldn't it be nice to be able to whistle up the assistance of a spirit which enabled you to start moving? A big hand please folks for the spirit GOFLOWOLFOG, the spirit who eases traffic blockages so that you can continue your journey. Goflowolfog typically appears in the form of a shades-wearing cat riding a skateboard. He brings with him a wind, and a noise which sounds like "Neeowww." He is of a cool, stylish disposition. Goflowolfog can be summoned when you are in a situation which falls under his governance, such as being stuck in a very crowded train (during a heat wave) which in accordance with the snafu principle, has stopped and shows no sign of moving again. In such a situation, listen out for the "Neeowww" and watch out for Goflowolfog as he zips past you on his skateboard, leaving the ghost-sensation of a breeze. If nothing else, this act of summoning may take your mind off sources of stress—such as the desire to murder the guy with the boom-box standing next to you as you slowly melt in the heat of the carriage. As the spirit slides past you, attract his attention by transforming yourself (if only inwardly) into a dude who is almost as cool and stylish as Goflowolfog himself, and visualise yourself for a moment standing with him on the skateboard as it flashes through the blockage. Then let go of the 'vision' and relax, allowing the spirit to get on with his job. If you should summon Goflowolfog to get the traffic around you moving, and he performs his task (even if you only move a few yards), then you are beholden to offer him something in return (it's only good manners). While there are many forms of appeasement to spirits, the two most pleasing to Goflowolfog are firstly, to allow someone else space to move. This could take the form of stepping back to let someone who is in a hurry walk past you, or allowing another car driver to move into your lane by leaving him a space. Secondly, be kind to the next cat you see. Where does Goflowolfog come from? He was identified and assembled during a magical seminar in London, on an evening when Britain was experiencing a heat wave, and everyone who had attended the seminar had experienced traffic problems in getting there. The design sequence was as follows:

1. *General Situation:* Traffic.

2. *Function Related to Situation:* Easing traffic stoppages.

3. *Naming the Spirit:* Several suggestions were made for an appropriate name, and GO FLOW was chosen. This name was made suitably 'barbaric' by *mirroring* it, thus GOFLOWOLFOG.

4. *Shape of the Spirit:* A number of possible shapes were suggested, such as a wheel or set of traffic signals, but the image of a cat riding a skateboard was both memorable, and similar to the bizarre incongruous shapes accorded to spirits in the Grimoires.

5. *Disposition or Character of the Spirit:* It was decided that Goflowolfog could be nothing but cool, stylish and relaxed, speedy and graceful. It was felt that he would respond kindly to anyone who attempted to take on these qualities in a situation as frustrating as being stuck in a traffic jam.

The sound associated with the movement of the spirit can also act as a mantra to help call him to you. His sigil, a circle containing two opposite-running arrows, can be used as a talisman, placed on cars, cycles or other modes of transport to draw the favour of Goflowolfog or as a focus for evocation. Using this process, you could easily create your own Grimoires of helpful spirits. It can be interesting (and fun!) to do this with a group of friends, so that not only are the spirits 'assembled' by many people, they are also used in different ways. The more successful usages of the spirit that are reported, the more 'confidence' in the spirit will be raised. Given time and wide usage, it may even happen that the image of your spirit enters the general cultural meme-pool. If you ever see a report in the *National Enquirer* or *Fortean Times* about sightings of cats riding skateboards, remember Goflowolfog!

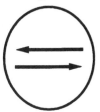

One of the consequences of this approach to working with Spirits is that it is easy to adopt the belief that 'spirits are everywhere.' There is a common tendency for magicians to fall into the trap of thinking that the various spirits—Gods, Demons, Allies, Faeries—can only be contacted in strictly magical situations and not at other times, and that they are there solely for our convenience and have no existence other than in our own heads. So what other forms and circumstances might have spirits associated with them? Again, I have begun to view some behaviors, attitudes, and beliefs as Spirits—in the sense of memes—ideas that take on an independent existence of those who carry them, and, in some senses, behave like viruses—propagating themselves through human hosts. I have, for example, considered 'Addiction' to be a Spirit, and have in one or two cases 'barred' the Spirit of heroin addiction from certain houses.

Another development of this approach has been to look at Tarot Cards as a structure for defining Spirits. I've often noted how two people can own the same deck of Tarot cards, yet each pack is subtly different from the other. When you get a new pack, it has a 'virgin' feel, and needs to be broken in. I've begun to look at well-used Tarot Packs as a collection of Spirits that arise from the user interacting with the cards. If you can adopt the belief that a Tarot card has a spirit attached, then by extrap-olation, it follows that *all* copies of that card in existence have some kind of spirit attached to them, and that you call 'summon' these spirits using your card.

Another point: we have been magically conditioned into thinking of Spirits in terms of the four classical elements—Fire, Water, Earth and Air. But what of the 'new' elements—petrol, electricity, nuclear power? What Spirits arise from these processes, and can we interact with them? That is for you to decide. So, all the cybernetic jargon I began this chapter with has led back to the classical Pantheist model of Spirits. They are everywhere, and they are 'independent' of us. Yet they arise, like the taste of sweetness from an apple, from our experience of the world, consciously or unconsciously. We may, to some extent, give them form and force by deciding that they are there—but often, once we have done so, then they stay there. Not so much in some murky 'astral' realm, but as part of the vast field of information through which we move.

CHAPTER SEVEN

EGO MAGIC

Our sense of being an individual emerges from clusters of beliefs, attitudes, self-definitions, inner conversations, boundaries and projections of 'otherness'. We move each day through a highly complex field of social relations, assuming roles, wearing carefully-crafted masks, and tacitly agreeing to play by the rules of Consensus, or Paramount Reality. Paramount Reality is a realm that has received very little attention, at least from a magical perspective. It is the reality that we move away from, and reluctantly return to, and is regarded by many as 'mundane' or 'material', as though it could not be a source of power or ecstasy. One of the strengths of Chaos Magic is the emphasis placed on identity work within the dimensions of Consensus Reality, dimensions which, after all, resemble the simplicities/ complexities of Fractals.

Some Chaos Magic exercises emphasise being able to adopt different belief systems, to change attitudes—not merely intellectually, but also in terms of emotional feelings and physical action. As in Tantric practice, we embrace that which we have rejected, and by so doing, push back the boundaries of what we consider possible. To do this successfully requires great determination, as entering a different belief system requires that we enter a new field of social relations, adopt new masks, accept new self-labels, and the behaviors and emotions that accompany them. Prolonged practice in such social paradigm shifting brings home one very clear point; that identity is fragile.

The sense of individual identity emerges from a complex series of interwoven social interactions. We internalise a series of self-labels and alliances, and from these arises our experience of selfhood. We may define ourselves in terms of work, status, race, nationality, or gender preference. Often, one particular set of social relations becomes the core of identity—the label which we fall back on to define ourselves to others as 'what we are'. As the patterns of post-industrial society become increasingly fractal in their behavior, so identity comes increasingly fluid—a position which implies both possibilities of freedom and great alienation and fear. As the fluctuations of social change become greater and greater, so there is an increased tendency to desire 'solid' connections with a historical past. Vide the obsessions with 'roots', 'getting back to nature' and the current vogue for cultural romanticism and invocation of 'Traditions'. All attempts to find points of anchorage; to create islands of order within what Austin Osman Spare called "the chaos of the normal."

Within the social maelstrom, many seek stability within subcultures, seeking to bolster up the sense of identity by merging with a group which has a clear 'style'—dress codes, beliefs, attitudes, emotive patterns, behaviors. Moving within the limited expressions of a distinct social system buffers us against chaos, and we can draw strength from the sense of being 'part' of a community, with varying degrees of a sense of 'separation' from 'mainstream' society. Magicians often report a growing sense of 'alien-ness' from consensus reality, a core perception which can all too easily manifest as ego-bound elitism or aloofness. How magicians deal with this experience of difference is thus, a source of great interest. This is particularly important within the Chaos and Tantric Paradigms, where the emphasis is on deconstructing identity rather than continually seeking to reinforce it through making stronger attachments to any one set of social relations, and thus limiting oneself to a particular range of expression and movement.

By entering a magical universe, we seek to impose order onto chaos. We enter Mythic Time, or Eternal Time—a link with the past through symbol, image, and continuity. An escape route, whereby we can gain a breathing space, a sense of order and continuity. There we can find identity, and root ourselves into a structure. The magical revival is powered by two related undercurrents. Firstly, the search for a personal and collective past, and secondly, the need for escape routes from the perceived tyranny of Paramount Reality. The desire to uncover and preserve the past is part of the impulse to preserve the self. Without knowing where we have been, it is difficult to know where we are going. The concern for uncovering the past, through ruins, museums, etc., has grown since the Nineteenth century. The past is the foundation of personal and collective identity. It offers the sense of continuity, of Eternal Time. But history is no longer truth. The past can be re-written, re-forged in a new image to feed our dreams of Golden Ages, of National Boundaries, of Ageless wisdom. History turns into commodity. The preoccupation with roots has grown rapidly since the 1970s, ever more so because of widespread insecurities in areas nominally seen as stable—labour, credit, technology, skills.

Magical universes return to us the promise of a meta-theory through which all things can be represented. This runs contrary to the spirit of the age, which turns increasingly away from global projections; where a meta-narrative is illusory. The sciences are suddenly uncertain; no longer able to chart the void through mathematics, they find smaller and smaller worlds to discover. The one-world dream of the Enlightenment is fragmenting, into worlds colliding and worlds apart; we don masks and enter the different reality-games, the social worlds layered through each other through which we pass each day. The alien worlds we glimpse reflected from the eyes of others whom we cannot touch; who's existence we can only guess at, refracted through the media net of stereotypes and labels. Images flicker across our eyes and in our heads. Becoming a magician, implies continual change, modification of identity, entering different paradigms of belief and behavior, learning new skills, and shedding life-patterns which have outworn their usefulness. There is thus a shift from a core 'Ego' which is based on maintaining differences the self-other divide, to that of 'Exo', the self in a continual process of dynamic engagement.

SELF-LOVE

The logical progression of this process is to reach the point where identity is continually being deconstructed—when a measure of fluidity of expression is attained and one is released from the necessity of having one's sense of self validated by others. This, is what Austin Osman Spare referred to when he wrote of his doctrine of "Self-Love." This is no narcissistic self-reflection of the glamours of the ego, rather, it is the void at the core of an identity which is freely able to move into any desired set of social relations, without becoming trapped or identified entirely within them. As the core of the sense of self is 'Self-love', rather than any label which encapsulates any particular set of behaviors, beliefs, and life-patterns, one attains a state of great freedom of movement and expression, without the need for self-definition. Self-love does not necessarily imply alienation or withdrawal from consensus reality. Modern culture is saturated with 'escape routes' by which we are encouraged to resist the routines of reality. Drugs, sex, fantasy scripts, communal living, separatist ideologies, therapies, mindscapes, and historical or utopian romanticism—all well-signposted escape routes that ultimately, can be shown to be dead-ends. This is especially true of revolutionary escape routes—political, lifestyles, or 'magical' endeavours. They support, rather than threaten, paramount reality, while feeding us the illusion that we are 'escaping'. Many of these escape routes require a change in social scripts and masks, and actually do little more than create temporary enclaves of activity within consensus reality. And consensus reality inevitably recaptures these enclaves—as seen when 'revolutions' inevitably become fashions and trends.

Magic is the great 'escape route'. Through its structures we can project ourselves into Mythic Time, make place and space sacred—project futures benign or otherwise. While political structures say 'change the structure and identity will change accordingly', magical realities emphasise 'change enough identity and the structure will follow'. Transient individualists all, we dream new towers from the bedrock of paramount reality. The difficulty comes when we need to convince others to share and support the dream. Thus the paradox of the current Aeon— personal identity has been rendered fluid, ephemeral, and endlessly open to the exercise of the will and imagination. This can be liberating. It is also, of course, deeply unsettling and stressful. Nostalgia for common values becomes a cultural force, as much for the counter-culture as the establishment. As our spatial and temporal worlds become increasingly compressed, so we respond with denial, cynicism or a blasé attitude to it all, sensory screening, yearning for a lost past, and the simplification of representation. The search for escape routes yields yet another market of commodities—drugs, sex, the occult, therapies, mindgames, politics. There is no escape from the Society of the Spectacle.

To understand the Chaoist approach to identity deconstruction we might look at the example of Aleister Crowley, who has left a good deal of useful material for exploring the boundaries of identity. Crowley's life can be understood as a continual battle between himself and consensus reality; a battle to create a personal enclave for himself beyond the limits of conventional morality. Crowley sought to escape from the Society of the Spectacle by becoming himself a Spectacle. He used his lovers, pupils and writings to create a free area in which he could express the myriad facets of selves which he had uncovered by his magical living. Crowley's approach to the problem of identity was an extreme one, and part of his drive towards the extremities of experience may have come from his desire to create a new society. Like many visionaries, he saw himself as the herald of a new phase of being for all humanity.

"Matter is my playground. I make and break without thought. Laugh and come UNTO me."
Eris, the Stupid Book

Modern society has exhorted the notion of individualism almost to a pathological degree. Within this urge to be individual are the continual demands to find 'real', 'higher' or 'true' selves. But if "Nothing is True" and "Everything is Permitted" we may come to discover that behind the masks and roles we slip into as we move through the social dynamics of Paramount Reality, there is only a whirling void. The Chaoist paradigm offers the freedom to be many individuals, and to find a sense of freedom, not through attempts to resist paramount reality or to create a free area beyond it, but to embrace it joyfully. While the majority of magical perspectives seek to transcend or reject Paramount Reality in favour 'higher' states of being, the Chaoist Paradigm makes Paramount Reality into a Playground for the phenomenizing of will and desire. By experiencing Paramount Reality from the basis of Self-Love, we begin the long and fascinating process of bringing to earth whatever shards of the future attract our gaze. By definition this is the activity of an elite group since few have the drive, stamina, and determination to continually strip away layers of identity in favour of freedom of movement.

BREAKING THE IMAGE

The Process of Deconditioning is very strongly emphasised within the Chaos Paradigm. Why? Essentially, this is a process of Self-Awareness—finding out 'who' you are, in terms of your acquired beliefs, attitudes, and patterns of behavior. As we move through life, so do we weave around ourselves a complex web of beliefs, self-identifications and internal conversations out of which arises that sense of being an individual which is generally called the Ego. Our sense of self is drawn from the 'solid' buildings of consensus reality—the patterns of thought, emotion, and behavior which form the basis of our interaction with the world, yet our sense of being a unique individual comes from the little ways in which we resist total assimilation into these structures. The Deconditioning Process is one which never ends, for even as we shake ourselves loose from limiting behaviors and beliefs, so too, we tend to form new ones.

It is relatively easy to reprogram 'magical beliefs'. This is not to say, however, that all belief-shifting is so simple. Some levels of our attitude/belief structure are remarkably resilient to conscious change. Indeed, some structures are able to 'resist' change by remaining elusive and 'invisible' to conscious awareness, and must be dragged, kicking, into the painful light of self-revelation. If I may use the analogy of beliefs as buildings (the city of Self), around the walls of which howls the wind of change, then the continual process of Deconditioning may be likened to chipping away at the towers, with the occasional 'tac-nuke' provided by recourse to a powerful form of gnosis such as sexual ecstasy, pain overload, or Albert Hoffman's elixir. Deconditioning is a continual process—even as you discard one set of limitations (in Tantra, this is known as Klesha-smashing), you may find that you acquire new ones, usually unconsciously. Often, belief-structures are 'nested' within each other, and may have their roots in a powerful formative experience. Timothy Leary calls this process 'Imprint Susceptibility', where the imprint forms a baseline response to experience, and establishes the parameters within which any subsequent learning takes place. Leary's 8-Circuit model of Metaprogramming can be employed as an aid to deconditioning.

Be mindful that the Deconditioning Process is not merely an intellectual experience. It is relatively easy to 'intellectually accept' some experience or belief which you have previously rejected or dismissed. It takes more resilience to take action from your new position, and risk the emotional upheaval that may result afterwards. For example, a young male magician of my acquaintance examined his own beliefs about his sexuality, and decided that he would focus upon his own distaste/fear of homoeroticism. He found that he could accept 'intellectually' his repressed attractions to other males, and thus thought himself liberated. He then went on to have several homosexual encounters which he said, did not give him any physical pleasure, but merely fed his 'belief' that he had sexually liberated himself. This kind of situation is all too easy to get caught up in. There is a common internal conversation which runs on the lines of "I am a magician, so I *ought* to be able to do anything without feeling guilt, nausea, uncomfortable" etc. This is merely another ego-identification which will give rise to intrapsychic contradictions. Habit and belief restructuring only tends to be successful when the desire to overcome a limitation is stronger than the desire to maintain it.

It is one thing to intellectually adopt different beliefs and attitudes, but quite another to live totally according to them. Our web of beliefs and attitudes quite often contradict each other at some level, and we don't tend to notice this until we begin the slow and painful process of self-examination. it's fairly easy, for example, to shift from being a 'fanatical' Christian to being a 'fanatical' magician. All that has shifted is the surface beliefs, the deep pattern of reinforcing an identity by rejecting anything that does not fit with the self-image remains. Deconditioning necessitates that the 'core' patterns—the threads around which we weave our self-image, be unpicked and untangled, that we understand how we have conditioned ourselves into a set of patterns for dealing with day-to-day experience. Some try and throw off all the shackles of conditioning at once, and declare themselves to be 'amoral'—which is often a self-deception in itself. So too, there are those who claim to have conquered the Ego—another fiction, since without a strong sense of personal identity, we are powerless to act, and magic is very much about doing.

One approach to Deconditioning is to adopt new 'masks'—to take on beliefs, attitudes, and identifications which are very much outside of your dominant self-image. Change your political ideas, shift from introvert to extrovert behavior, shed established habits and addictions (a feat in itself!) and adopt new ones, modify your range of sexual behavior, consciously adopt new gestures and body postures, or become passionate about things you would normally dismiss as 'trivial'. In the cultural melting-pot of modern society, it is possible to move through a myriad of subcultures, each with its own attitudes, beliefs, ways of defining reality, and social codes. But be warned, you can't get out of bed one morning and say, 'today I'm going to be a hedonistic, pleasure-seeking Satanist.' Belief-shifting takes time—time, and the investment of emotional energy and determination. Also, it's too easy to merely belief-shift within the safety of your own head—you must wear this new mask continually within that most difficult realm—the world of social relations. You may take it as a sign of success when other people are convinced by your new identity, and accept you (or reject you) on that basis. One of the resultant insights from belief shifting in this way is that of empathy—being able to understand another person's world-view. It is also instructive to realise that your beliefs, when compared to those who you once considered as diametrically opposed to you, are equally nonsensical. Cynical, perhaps? Well, I prefer to see this as a form of liberation. if 'Nothing Is True', then you might as well adopt new selves and beliefs with joy, knowing that, while your wear them, they are as 'true' as anything else.

Deconditioning is rarely simple. Often people who have had an experience of 'Illumination' report that all their old repressive structures have dropped away. Tear down a building in the city of identities and it grows back, sometimes with a different shape. One of the effects of intense Gnosis is the shattering of layers of belief structure, but it is generally found that unless follow-up work is done, the sense of shattered belief-structures is transitory. You should also consider the effects this process is likely to have on others—see Luke Rhinehart's *The Dice Man* for an amusing and instructive tale of one man's approach to deconditioning. The Ego, a self-regulatory structure which maintains the fiction of being a unique self, doesn't like the process of becoming more adaptive to experience. One of the more subtle 'defenses' that it throws up is the sneaking suspicion (which can quickly become an obsession) that you are 'better' than everyone else. In some circles, this is known as 'Magusitis', and it is not unknown for those afflicted to declare themselves to be Maguses, Witch Queens, avatars of Goddesses, or Spiritual Masters. If you catch yourself referring to everyone else as 'the herd', or 'human cattle', etc., then it's time to take another look at where you're going. Myself, I prefer the benefits of empathy and the ability to get on with other people than the limitations of being a reclusive would-be Raskalnikov dreaming of the serving slaves. While we might echo the words of Hassan I Sabbah that "Nothing is True, Everything is Permitted", acting totally from this premise is likely to bring you into conflict with those individuals and authorities who have pretty fixed views on what isn't permitted. Thus, despite the glamour, Chaos Magicians are rarely completely amoral. One of the basic axioms of magical philosophy is that morality grows from within, once you have begun to know the difference between what you have learned to believe, and what you will to believe.

CHARTING THE SELF

Here are some preliminary exercises in Self-Examination. All they require is the honesty not to flinch from those parts of ourselves which we find unpalatable.

1. Third Person

Write an account of yourself written in the third person—as though another person were writing about you. Discuss your relative strengths and weaknesses, as though you were writing a work reference for yourself.

2. Lists

Divide a sheet of paper into two halves. On one side, list your 'strengths', and on the other, your 'weaknesses'. To go further, you could consider 'Life Successes' and 'Life Failure', Fears and Fantasies. Continue, by listing 'things' which attract you, and that which repels you.

3. A Book Of Blunders

Find a blank book, and pour into it every instance in your life which you have found emotionally painful, feel 'guilty' about, or embarrassing. The idea is not to try and 'rise above' such events, or to wallow in self-pity, but to gain an honest catalogue of 'negative' events which lurk in your personal past.

4. Suppressions

Again, try to compile a list of those aspects of your self which you struggle, to varying degrees, to repress. Fears, fantasies, desires, 'mad' thoughts, etc.

5. Conversations

A good deal of our self-image is woven from the 'internal' conversations we have with ourselves. Stories which we tell ourselves about what we can, and can't do, or could do, if only... Identifying these conversations and how we uphold them, is another step towards self-awareness.

6. Destroying The Stereotype

When you encounter someone who provokes your tendency to label them as an example of a stereotype—hippy, red-neck, skinhead, fag etc., quickly fire 'alternative' suggestions to yourself about why that person might look as they do. See how many alternative identifications you can come up with for an individual.

7. Storytelling

Watch other people in a room talking. How many 'stories' can you create around them? Are the couple in the corner talking conspiracy, business, extra-marital affair?

PATTERN RECOGNITION

As we move through life we tend to develop habituated patterns of thought and behavior. One area of experience where these patterns can be dysfunctional is in relationships. For example, if you have become used to an 'open' relationship with a partner, you might find a partner's desire that you become monogamous a restriction upon your sense of freedom. It is common to take habituated patterns of adaptation and survival across relationships, often to the detriment of new situations. Obviously, identifying these patterns is useful, particularly as we tend to hold onto them without realising that they are no longer viable.

OBSESSIONAL DEMONS

We are bound by our own past, bound to repeat patterns; programs written long ago. Flowcharted in an infant's crabbed hand; meshed like kitten-pulled wool; a language of critical moments in our personal histories. Years later, a gap opens in the world, and creatures of free will and freedom that we think we are, our sudden vulnerability surprises us. Caught off guard we pause, and in that silence, ancient-innocent fingers deep within us pluck at strings, so that we jerk awkwardly in the grip of self-spawned monsters of the mind—obsessions.

DEFENSE MECHANISMS

The more value that we place on upholding a particular emotional pattern, the more likely it is that all ambiguous signals will be perceived as supporting it. Evidence which counters it will most likely be overlooked or rationalised into a more malleable form. Conflict arises when dissonance occurs between desires and existing mental constructs (have you ever feared the strength of your own desires?). To cope with such conflicts, a variety of Defense Mechanisms can be adopted:

Aggression

A typical response to frustrated desire and loss of control; loss of devouring dreams. We can direct it at the source of our frustration, or direct it onto others.

Apathy

Loss of control—loss of face and self-worth. The machine stops.

Regression

Adult, who me? A return to a child-like mien. Cry hard enough and someone will come and comfort us. Perhaps we have learned that through tears, we can control others.

Sublimation

In other words, putting a brave face on it. Re-directing the energy into a more acceptable form. But demons are cunning. Kick them down the front stairs and they will come sneaking round the back, waiting with spider calm until you leave the door of your mind ajar.

Intellectualisation

Displacing feelings with words. A quick lie for the aesthetic becomes a fast buck for the lay analyst.

Such strategies are normal; that is until they become obsessive: a locked-up loop automatic as breathing. Out of control.

FANTASY

Fantasy is the cornerstone of obsession, where imagination is trussed up like a battery-farmed chicken; catharsis eventually becomes catastrophic. Walter Mitty lives in all of us, in varyingly-sized corners. We use "starter" fantasies to weave meaning into a new situation, "maintainer" fantasies to prop up a boring task, and "stopper" fantasies to persuade ourselves that it's better not to...

A fantasy has tremendous power, and in a period of high anxiety we can imagine a thousand outcomes, good and bad (but mostly good) of what the dreaded/hoped for moment will bring us.

The fantasy exists in a continual tension between the desire to fulfill it, and the desire to maintain it—to keep from losing it. Of course, any move to realise it threatens its existence. A closed loop is the result, shored up by our favourite defense mechanisms, whipped on by fear of failure and lust of result. The obsession clouds all reason, impairs the ability to act, makes anything secondary to it seem unimportant. It's a double-bind tug o'war. The desire to maintain the fantasy may be stronger than the desire to make it real.

In classical occult terms I am describing a thought-form, a monster bred from the darker recesses of mind, fed by psychic energy, clothed in imagination and nurtured by umbilical cords which twist through years of growth. We all have our personal Tunnels of Set; set in our ways through habit and patterns piling on top of each other. The thought-form rides us like a monkey; its tail wrapped firmly about the spine of a self lost to us years ago; an earlier version threshing blindly in a moment of fear, pain, or desire. Thus we are formed; and in a moment of loss we feel the monster's hot breath against our backs, its claws digging into muscle and flesh. we dance to the pull of strings that were woven years ago, and in a lightning flash of insight, or better yet, the gentle admonitions of a friend, we may see the lie; the program. It is first necessary to see that there is a program. To say perhaps, this creature is mine, but not wholly me. What follows then is that the prey becomes the hunter, pulling apart the obsession, naming its parts, searching for fragments of understanding in its entrails. Shrinking it, devouring it, peeling the layers of onion-skin.

This is in itself a magic as powerful as any sorcery. Unbinding the knots that we have tied and tangled; sorting out the threads of experience and colour-coding the chains of chance. It may leave us freer, more able to act effectively and less likely to repeat old mistakes. The thing has a Chinese puzzle-like nature. We can perceive only the present, and it requires intense sifting through memory to see the scaffolding beneath. The grip of obsession upon us has three components:

Cognitive—our thoughts and feelings in relation to the situation. These must be ruthlessly analysed and cut down by self-assessment, banishing, or some similar strategy.

Physiological—anxiety responses of heart rate, muscle tone and blood pressure. The body must be stilled by relaxation and meditation.

Behavioral—what we must do (or more often, not do). Often our obsessive behavior is entirely inappropriate and potentially damaging to others. Usually it takes other people to point this out. Analytic techniques such as I Ching or Tarot may be useful.

BREAKING BOUNDS

A simple, yet effective approach to Ego Magic is to use a positive ego-identification to overcome a negative ego-identification. For example, I hate mathematics. As a teenager, I often cut school classes in mathematics and would go to any lengths to avoid anything which involved algebra or logical formulas. According to a child psychologist I had developed a mathematics 'block' which has, up until recently, remained pretty unshakable. The "I know I cannot do mathematical things" self-statement is the negative ego-identification here. My example of a positive ego-identification is "I can get computers to do what I want them to." Since moving to my present company, I have gained the reputation for being the person to ask about computer problems, mainly due to the fact that I read the manuals, experiment with the programs and like customising them when allowed. The two ego-identifications came together quite suddenly when I was asked to develop a series of databases to cover a series of tasks. This was no problem initially, but suddenly I found that I had to set up mathematical formula for calculating Value Added Tax or differing percentage discounts on products. Here, the two ego-identifications came into direct conflict. I should point out that my awareness that this was the case arose gradually through the task, and in the end, the stronger of the two was the identification that I can make computers do things, which has in turn, weakened my resistance to mathematical things. This is not so much a conscious process of setting one identification against another, but more of becoming aware of what is happening during such a transaction. The breaking of such conditioned 'barriers' can be observed when an individual assumes a sexual identity—particularly if the identity has been associated with negative conditioning—such as being homosexual or a transvestite. There is usually a conflict between one's own perceived 'nature', negative ego-conditioning, and the desire to act upon the basis of self-identification. So the self-statement "Am I really one of those" becomes associated with both desire and self-loathing.

MANY SELVES

One idea that is becoming more popular, is the concept of the legion of Selves—something that both New Agers and Chaos Magicians find attractive. Rather than pursuing the dualistic fondness for higher and lower selves, egos and superegos, etc., there is the idea that we are a multiplicity of identities out of which the sense of self-identity emerges. A similar idea exists in some Tantric philosophies—that Shiva (Consciousness) is surrounded by a 'bag' of Shaktis, but that he's not fucking all of them at once. Here, the approach is to identify the different selves, and give them all, as your situation befits, a turn at being the one which is the 'seat' of identity. It can be helpful to define a number of distinct personalities which you can flip in and out of as the need arises.

THE NEUTRAL SELF

You hold yourself as slightly distant and aloof from other people, so that you can observe them covertly, finding out their strengths and weaknesses. You are quiet and economical in your movements. Every word you speak is measured and you are not given to verbosity by any means. You rarely demonstrate disapproval or, for that matter, approval, and seem to accept other people's behavior as a matter of course.

FREEDOM OF BELIEF

One aspect of Chaos Magic that seems to upset some people is the Chaos Magician's (or Chaoist, if you like) occasional fondness for working with images culled from non-historical sources, such as invoking H. P. Lovecraft's Cthulhu Mythos beings, mapping the Rocky Horror Show onto the Tree of Life, slamming through the astral void in an X-Wing fighter, and 'channeling' communications from gods that didn't exist five minutes ago. So you might see why using this sort of thing as a basis for serious magical work raises one or two eyebrows in some quarters. Isn't after all, the Lovecraft stuff fiction? What about linking in with 'inner planes contacts', 'traditions', etc.— surely you can't do magic with something that doesn't bear any relation to history or mythology? In the past, such criticisms have been raised over the subject of magicians working with 'fictional' entities. In this section, I hope to argue the case against these objections.

The first point to make is that magic requires a belief system within which we can work. The belief system is the symbolic and linguistic construct through which the magician learns to interpret her experiences and can range from anything between good old traditional Qabalah to all this New Age "I-heard-it-off-a-Red-Indian-Shaman-honest" stuff that seems so popular nowadays. It doesn't matter which belief system you use, so long as it turns you on. Read that again, it's important. Eventually most magicians seem to develop their own magical systems which work fine for them but are a bit mind boggling for others to use. Austin Osman Spare's Alphabet of Desire is a good example. A key to magical success is veracity of belief. If you want to try something out, and can come up with a plausible explanation as to how/why it should work, then it most likely will. Pseudoscience or Qabalistic gibber (or both)—it matters not so long as the rationale you devise buffers the strength of your belief in the idea working. I find that this happens a lot when I try to push the limits of some magical action I haven't tried before. Once I come up with a plausible explanation of how it could work in theory, then, of course, I am much more confident about doing and can often transmit this confidence to others. If I'm 110% certain that this ritual's going to 'bloody well work' then it's all the more likely that it will. You can experiment with this using the technique of belief-shifting or metaprogramming—for example, use the chakras. The popular view of chakras is that we have seven. Okay, so meditate on your chakras, hammer the symbolism into your head and hey presto! you'll start having seven-Chakra experiences. Now switch to using the five Sephiroth of Israel Regardie's Middle Pillar (Qabalah) as the psychic centres in your body, and sure enough, you'll get accordant results. Get the idea? Any belief system can be used as a basis for magic, so long as you can invest belief into it. Looking back at my earlier magical experiments, I guess that what used to be important for me was the strong belief that the system I was using was ancient, based on traditional formulae, etc. A belief system can be seen as a matrix of information into which we can pour emotional energy—we do as much when we become so engrossed in watching a play, film, or TV programme that, for a moment, it becomes real for us, and invokes appropriate emotions. Much of what we see on the silver screen is powerful mythic images and situations, repackaged for modern tastes, which is a cue to start going on about *Star Trek*.

More people are familiar with the universe of *Star Trek* than any of the mystery religions. It's a safe bet that more people know who Mr. Spock is than know who Lugh is. The *Star Trek* universe has a high fantasy content, and seemingly few points of contact with our 'everyday' worlds of experience. Yet *Star Trek* is a modern, mythic reflection of our psychology. The characters embody specific qualities—Spock is logical, Sulu is often portrayed as a martial figure, Scotty is a 'master builder', and Kirk is an arbitrator. As we "get into" the *Star Trek* universe, we find greater depth and subtlety. We find that the universe has its own rules which the characters are subject to, and is internally consistent. In each episode we may find that we are being given insights into the Personal world of a key character. Like our everyday worlds, the universe of *Star Trek* has a boundary beyond which is the unknown—the future, unexplored space, the consequences of our actions—whatever wild cards that we may be dealt. So we watch and enter, as an observer, the unfolding of a Mythic event. We can increase this sense of participation through a role-playing game, where group belief allows us to generate, for a few hours at least, the semblance of the *Star Trek* universe, in the comfort of our sitting room. It's relatively easy to generate the *Star Trek* world, due to the plethora of books, comics, videos and role-playing supplements which are available to support that universe. One of my colleagues had to sit for a computer exam, and was wracking his brains trying to think of an appropriate god-form to invoke to concentrate his mind on programming. Mercury? Hermes? And then he hit on it—the most powerful mythic figure that he knew that could deal with computers was—Mr. Spock! So he proceeded to learn all he could about Spock and went around saying "I never will understand humans" until he was thoroughly Spock-ified. The result he achieved in the examination was higher than he otherwise would have expected. And so, back to the Cthulhu Mythos. Lovecraft himself believed that fear, particularly fear of the unknown, was the strongest emotion attached to the Great Old Ones. I like to work with that Mythos occasionally because the Great Old Ones are 'outside' most human mythologies, reflecting the shadows of the Giants in Norse Myths, the pre-Olympian Titans in Greek Myths, and other groups of universe-builders who are thought to be too chaotic for the polite company of the gods of the ordered universe. For me, too, the nature of the Great Old Ones as shadowy beings who can only be partially glimpsed is attractive—they can't be assimilated and bound into any orthodox systems of magic and I get much fun from working out suitable approaches for working with them. The Great Old Ones have a very 'primal' nature, which for me provides the emotional buffer for magical exploration. Having said all that, and perhaps left you thinking "uurgh, weird person, he likes messing round with tentacled slimies," I might also mention that I've had some interesting results from working with a Mythic system based on (blush) C. S. Lewis's 'Narnia' books.

The interesting thing about metaprogramming is that you can adopt a belief for a relatively short time, and then drop it again. When practising ritual magic it's generally a good idea to behave as if gods are real—whatever you think about their being archetypes or reflections of bits of yourself or whatever. So in a Cthulhu Mythos ritual, nothing will help build the necessary tension than the adopted belief that if you get it wrong Cthulhu will slime you! Of course, outside the ritual you don't have to believe in Cthulhu and that even now a slimy paw appears at my window...no! No!...ahem, sorry about that. Related to this is the idea that 'Suspension of Disbelief' can also be useful. To do this take a book which expounds an idea that you find totally crap (every magician has their favourite 'crap' author) and try to see the writer's message without your inner voice hurling abuse at the page. One of the most difficult 'suspensions' for fledgling magicians is overcoming the nagging doubt that "all this stuff doesn't work." Despite hours of talk and reading vast tomes by Crowley et. al., that nagging disbelief can still be heard, and can only be dispelled by experience—one act that shows you that MAGIC WORKS is worth a thousand arguments. Intensity of belief is the key which allows magical systems to work, whether they are related to historical traditions (which are, let's face it, often rewritten anyway), esoteric traditions (which have evolved down the centuries as well) or based on fiction or TV. It's your ability to be emotively moved or to use them as vehicles for the expression of your will that counts. If it works for you—do it.

CHAPTER EIGHT

KALI IN THE DISCO

A good example of practical magic in action involved a friend of mine who wanted to increase her power of attraction for other women by working with a particular Goddess. She decided that Kali, the Hindu Goddess of sex and death was the mythic figure who represented the qualities she wanted to boost in herself, so we worked out a Pathworking where she merged with a modern-day image of Kali, and strode, chains rattling, into the women's disco, laser-beam eyes sweeping the crowd at the bar, who were naturally awestruck by her poise and all-round power. On one level, this is no more than what adolescents do when modeling a culture hero—imagining themselves to be that person, and thereby gaining a little of their power. All Gods and Goddesses are personifications of physical and mental attributes which we can engender in ourselves by a variety of techniques—collectively known as Invocation—the process where we identify ourselves, for a time, with a mythic figure to such an extent that we gain access to abilities and qualities associated with that entity.

Invocation is one of the most widely used of magical techniques, and to get the best from it, requires some ability in visualisation, use of voice, awareness of the use of posture and gesture, kinesthetic memory, practice in the various routes into gnosis, relaxation, and self-awareness. Of course, performing invocations is a very practical way of developing these skills.

WHY INVOKE?

The benefits of boosting one's confidence and poise, by identifying with a larger-than-life (mythic) figure, should be obvious from the opening anecdote. By using invocatory techniques, you can give more prominence to a shadow-self by bringing it into full awareness. You can invoke an entity about which you know comparatively little, in order to gain insights into its nature and character. Another use of invocation is to 'boost' your capacity to perform other acts of magic. Acts of sorcery, for example, can be performed following the invocation of an appropriate entity which allows you to feel charged with power and single-minded to a supernormal degree. Information may be sought via the invocation of a deity who's province is oracles. Invocation is a further demonstration of the operation of controlled feedback to alter the perception of your immediate reality. Basically, you are using a combination of techniques to reinforce the belief that you are becoming someone or something 'other' than your dominant self-perception. How is this done? The best way to illustrate this process is by way of an example. Ra-Hoor-Khuit is an Egyptian deity who is an aspect of the hawk-headed god, Horus. He is of some significance within the magical paradigm of Thelema, which has evolved out of the magical work of Aleister Crowley. Among other things, he is described as the god of "strength and silence." He appears as a hawk, or as a hawk-headed man. Ra-Hoor Khuit is generally associated with martial prowess. He is a warrior-god, but we can gain a further insight into his nature by looking at the qualities of a hawk. A hawk is powerful, aggressive and predatory, but in a very controlled sense. It hovers high above the land, until it spots its prey, whereon it swoops in for the kill. Ra-Hoor Khuit also has solar associations, and a powerful representation of him is the 'Aeon' card in the Crowley-Harris Thoth deck. So, when invoking Ra-Hoor-Khuit, we are identifying with these qualities; the power, confidence and poise of the god, the perceptual acuity of the hawk, and also a sense of freedom and detachment from the object (target) of our will.

A first step in this direction might be to perform a Pathworking, which enables us to attune ourselves to the appro-priate 'ambiance' for invoking Ra-Hoor-Khuit.

RA-HOOR-KHUIT PATHWORKING

This Pathworking should be prefaced with a relaxation exercise. It should be done in a position which allows you to be relaxed and attentive to the narrative. For best results, read it onto a cassette recorder. You are beginning to relax—listen to my voice and let yourself be carried along—feel yourself drifting in darkness, and slowly become aware of a gentle rocking sensation...

You find yourself sitting upright in a boat—the wide, blue waters of the Nile stretch before you. The sky is bright blue above your head, and you can feel the warm rays of the noonday sun about you. A cool breeze wafts from the sails as the ship drifts down the winding river. In the prow of the boat stands the tall figure of a man with the head of a long-beaked bird—it is the god THOTH, your guide on this journey.

As you drift along, you can see people walking along the palm-bordered banks of the river, and glimpse the tall columns of some distant temple. Ahead of you, rising over the dunes, you can see the apex of some mighty pyramid—your destination.

Now your craft is gliding to rest by a wooden jetty. Thoth gestures with his right hand, silently pointing you on your way. You clamber out of the boat and ahead, you see the path to the pyramid, a stone-paved avenue, guarded by a statue of the inscrutable sphinx. You walk slowly towards the sphinx and pause briefly, reflecting on its four magical powers: to Know, to Will, to Dare, and to Keep Silent. For a moment, it seems that the sphinx's stone gaze is testing your resolve, and then the spell breaks and you continue on your way. You walk slowly along the stone path, feeling the heat of the stones against your feet, until you reach the foot of the pyramid.

The entrance is above you, high in the side of the pyramid; a dark yawning archway, at the top of a staircase of marble. You ascend the steps, feeling the rays of the sun against your back. You reach the archway, and you see that it is decorated with the image of Khephra, the Scarab Beetle who carries the sun through the darkness. The archway is veiled with a curtain of purple, flecked with silver. You raise your hands to part it, and step through onto the other side.

You are standing in a dark, cool passage, which slopes down-wards. All is silent and still, and your breath seems to echo around the stone, so that you touch your fingers to your lips, as if to hush the air escaping. Once more firm in your resolve, you begin to walk down into the bowels of the ancient tomb. Although the passageway is dark, you begin to see the way ahead, illuminated by a strange, starry radiance which dimly glows about you. You can feel the weight of the centuries pressing upon you as you walk, so that your own sense of time passing is clouded—it feels as though you have been walking down this passage for millennia.

And then the starry glow reveals an archway ahead. A pair of scales hangs above it—the symbol of judgement. You pause for a moment, mindful of the fate of those who are tried and found wanting. Gathering up your courage, you step inside the archway. A black feather falls at your feet, and you bend down to pick it up. As you stand up, you see that you have entered a temple.

The temple has four square, stone walls. The ceiling glows with the radiance of the night sky, filled with stars. The floor is composed of alternating tiles of silver and gold. In the centre, close to where you are standing, is an altar. It is shaped in the form of a double cube, made of brass. Upon the altar is a small green cross and a single red rose. In the east quarter of the temple, there is a solid green throne. The air in the temple seems charged with energy, yet it is calming and soothing. It fills you with feelings of power and joy. You rest here awhile, immersing yourself in the force of he who resides here, the hawk-headed lord, Ra-Hoor-Khuit.

You look down and study the black feather in your hand, and you silently repeat the name RA-HOOR-KHUIT. As you repeat the name, the air about you seems to shimmer, and you are surrounded by a golden radiance, speckled with stars of deepest black. You feel that the radiance is spreading through your body, and you can feel a tingling, as tiny motes of gold shimmer all over your body. You turn once more to the throne, and now, seated upon it, it a large, regal figure. He has the body of a tall, powerfully-built man, but with the head of a hawk. You are in the presence of Ra-Hoor-Khuit, the lord of the Aeon. He notices you, and fixes you with his gaze. His eyes seem to burn into the very core of your being. He speaks:

> I am the Hawk-Headed Lord of Silence and of Strength;
> my nemyss shrouds the night-blue sky. I am the Lord of
> the Double Wand of Power; the wand of the force of
> Coph Nia—but my left hand is empty, for I have crushed
> an universe; and nought remains.

The fire behind his eyes leaps higher, and you feel yourself tremble, almost in fear. The god rises and raises his arms—his hands stretch out towards you. Energy flows from his outstretched fingertips—a constant stream of force directed into your heart. You rock back on your heels as the energy floods into your being—inflaming your spirit with the divine essence of Ra-Hoor-Khuit.

The world seems to spin around you—you have fleeting visions of what you might accomplish with this power. Then the flood is stilled, and once more Ra-Hoor-Khuit is seated before you. A single star now hangs above the altar, the symbol of your aspiration. You raise your fingers to your lips in reverence, and feel your body glowing with silent strength. You can see now that each of the four walls about you has an archway in its centre, and you realise that you are standing at the crossroads of the Universe. You rest awhile, preparing yourself to go once more into the world. You are calm, yet you feel the energy within as a leaping flame within your breast. You hold up the black feather and offer a silent prayer of thanks to Ra-Hoor-Khuit. You feel yourself drawn into the golden radiance and you are transported across time and space. There is a moment of blackness, and then, in your own time, you can open your eyes and stretch your limbs. You have returned.

Performing this Pathworking will allow you to 'get the feel' of the qualities and feelings associated with Ra-Hoor-Khuit. Having experienced his power in this way, the next step is to draw it into yourself.

Determine your intent and state it clearly. An appropriate Statement of Intent for Ra-Hoor-Khuit might be: "It is my Will to invoke Ra-Hoor-Khuit, for magical power and the vision to see my next step on the path."

THE ASSUMPTION OF GOD-FORMS

This is a simple technique for identifying yourself with a chosen deity. Stand up, and find a posture which for you represents relaxed preparation for action. Visualise Ra-Hoor-Khuit standing behind you. Breathe deeply and slowly, and with each breath let the sensations, memories and feelings you experienced in the Pathworking well up. Feel his terrible gaze upon your back. Feel the power of his presence behind you. When you can stand this pressure no longer, imagine Ra-Hoor-Khuit stepping forwards, as he did in the Pathworking, but into your body. You stretch your arms out in front of you, and feel the power and force of the god flooding into you. Let your body outline become his, and feel his power as yours, so that you feel supercharged with energy, yet calm and distant. Repeat the speech that Ra-Hoor-Khuit gave in the Pathworking.

In respect of your statement of intent, you should first feel charged with confidence and power, and then, while experiencing this state of awareness, you can examine your magical work, and make a firm decision as to what you will do next. To 'earth' yourself following the invocation, you could give a short prayer of thanks to Ra-Hoor-Khuit, and perform a short visualisation which separates yourself from the god. An example of this is to visualise the god transforming into a hawk, and flying into the sun. As you do this, the sensations you feel change to a sense of peaceful calm, and a sense of accomplishment that you achieved your purpose. The departed god is carrying the seed of your will into the future, and you may now banish and go forth.

INVOCATION AS DRAMA

Invocation and acting have a lot in common. Indeed it is sometimes appropriate to think of ritual invocation as a performance aimed at the entity you are attempting to invoke. If you put on a good performance you will be rewarded. Blow your lines and you won't be asked to come back for a second season. I often find it useful to watch actors or comedians on television, particularly to look at their posture, use of gesture, and voice. These three abilities are powerful ways of communicating nuances of mood and expression, and play a key role in the theatre of magic.

USE OF VOICE

It's not so much, what you say, but *how* you say it; in other words, the *Structure* of the invocation. Classical magical invocations have three parts to them. First the deeds and history of the entity are spoken of—in the third person. Then the qualities of the entity are spoken of—in the second person. And finally, the powers of the entity are given, in the first person, so that you gradually identify yourself with the entity. An example might be:

1) "Wolf, who ate Red Riding Hood's grandmother, I invoke you."

2) "You who have the big eyes, the hairy pelt, the terrible teeth, I invoke you."

3) "I am the big bad wolf, ravenous and hungry, keen-eyed and cunning."

Get the idea?

Further, to make effective use of the voice, you need to be aware of two aspects of voice technique: Rhythm and Delivery.

Rhythms carry our consciousness along, from heartbeats, to cycles of breathing, sleeping, night-day and the passage of seasons. rhythms promote associated body movements and adjustments, and act as a signal to begin movement without conscious effort, so that less energy is expended when you begin; for example, it has been shown that soldiers can march further, with less fatigue, when accompanied by a marching band. The feeling of being "carried" comes from the structure that rhythm gives to our time-sense, and the pattern gives a sense of continuance. It becomes a motor attitude, and one's attention is freed (if this is desired). Rhythms are everywhere around us, and chants and songs reflect this fact and bring us towards an enhanced sense of participation in the world.

During invocation, the way in which we deliver speech is different from our usual habits of talking in that there may be an enhanced deliberateness in our enunciations, or greater care taken in projecting the subtle nuances of emotion—awe, ecstasy, gentleness or martial prowess. Whether our words well up, unbidden, from the Deep Mind, or have been carefully linked together in prolonged brainstorming sessions, it is highly likely that we will try and find a certain distinct rhythm around which to frame our words.

The Deep Mind often speaks to us in verse. Cross-cultural studies of the vocal patterns of people in the throes of possession show a striking similarity: a rising and falling intonation at the end of each phrase, each phrase punctuated by a pause or groan. This pattern emerges regardless of native language and cultural background. The English version of this rhythm is known as Iambic Pentameter. You can hear it in the frenzied oratorical deliveries of evangelical preachers and in the apparently meaningless gush of words from those who have been seized by the 'Holy Spirit'. It wells forth from the Deep Mind as unconscious or deity-inspired poetry and communications.

As the Deep Mind calls to us with a particular rhythm and meter, so do we attempt to call into the depths of our being by rhythmically pulsing our speech. Sound, like light, sets up rhythms in our brains, as experiments with electro-encephalographs (EEGs) have shown. These internal rhythms reflect the sounds which propel us into varying degrees of trance, whether it is the gentle, watery lapping of the Moon or the thundering frenzy of Pan. If we are caught off guard, and susceptible, their effect can be devastating. When designing invocations, rhythm and delivery should be considered. If you design a verbal invocation for Ra-Hoor-Khuit, you would consider how you want the qualities and power of the god to be reflected in your voice. A strong, martial rhythm might be appropriate, perhaps repetitive, calm and confident, with a sense of gathering power. How do you think the god would speak? It's a safe bet that he wouldn't mumble, stammer or say "er..." between sentences.

Some beautiful invocations appear in magical textbooks—but the best kind of invocation is the one that works for you. Words spoken confidently, from the heart, will be more effective than half-remembered lines from a book. Although you can get good results reading invocations, unless you have a lectern to put the book on, it is difficult to wave your hands around, which can negate the use of gesture to reinforce what you are saying.

Gestures and postures reinforce other elements of invocation. A key element of invocatory practice is learning to associate postures and gestures with appropriate emotions and sensations. The use of postural shifts is fairly easy to grasp.

THE NEUTRAL POSTURE

Find a posture which, for you, reflects a sense of calm readiness for action. You should be relaxed, attentive to what is around you, and prepared (but not *tensed*) for whatever is going to happen next. You should be able to find both a standing and a sitting posture. Lying down is *not* recommended though, as it is difficult to spring into action from a prone position. This posture represents you at your *Axis Mundi* , the mind at rest.

Finding this posture is useful as it is the posture which you can move in and out of to demarcate between different magical acts. For example, in the Assumption of God-Forms described above, you would move out of this posture and take on the posture of the entity you are invoking upon yourself, and back into it, when you have finished.

How might your body posture change when you invoke an entity into yourself? Most entities have characteristic postures. However, if you don't its a characteristic posture, you can decide on one in advance. As you experience a change in perception, your body posture will change in ways of which you may not (at first) be wholly aware. An enhanced feeling of confidence and poise tends to draw your shoulders back and your head up. Your chest cavity will expand as you breathe deeply and slowly; your limbs will be further away from the centerline of your body. Standing with your feet apart and your arms spread upwards and outwards, for example, is the classical posture for invocation—you are extending your body space to its limits, making yourself vulnerable. Conversely, standing with your arms folded across your chest, and your head bent slightly downwards is the classical posture for 'closing' after works of magic, as you close yourself off to external influences.

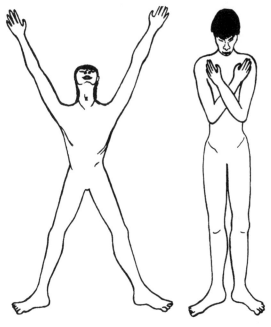

Gestures are a key element in non-verbal communication, with a wide range of uses from making a simple, yet emphatic, gesture at the motorist who overtakes you, to the elaborate signing languages used by those with impaired speech. The gesture which is used most in modern magic is that of jabbing one's dominant hand sharply outwards from the shoulder, representing the magical will projecting forth into the future.

Experiment with using gestures until you find ones which for you, eloquently communicate relaxation, drawing inwards, projecting forth power, and so on. For example, cupping one's hands can signify the gathering of power. Focus awareness into your hands and feel a faint tingling sensation, and a slight resistance when you try and bring them together. Imagine a ball of energy forming in this space, and imagine a sigil forming in its' midst. Take a deep breath, clap your hands loudly and make a gesture of flinging outwards. A very simple way of casting an enchantment. Find others, and create your own battery of gestures.

MASK MAGIC

In modern Western culture, masks are reduced to objects of art, to be hung on walls or displayed in museums. At best they are used as disguises.

In surviving shamanic cultures however, masks are considered to be extremely powerful magical weapons. Some African tribes, for example, keep their masks locked away, to protect people from the power of the masks gaze. Some Polynesian masks are carved with their eyes looking downwards, so they cannot stare directly at onlookers.

A mask hung on a wall may be beautiful to look at, but has very little vitality until its "personality" has been activated. Both tribal shamans and modern drama teachers impress on their students that *masks have their own personalities.* When a mask is donned, the personality of the wearer is overshadowed by that of the mask, and once the wearer becomes used to this idea, a trance state may ensue where the "spirit" of the mask takes over.

As a magical object, the purpose of the mask is to drive out the individual's personality, and allow a "spirit" to take over. Both overshadowing and full possession may be experienced in working with masks. It's not so much that you wear the mask, but that *the mask wears your body*. It is the mask that is responsible for what happens, rather than the wearer.

Mask teacher Keith Johnstone emphasises that masks do not, at first, have access to their bodies skills, nor can they talk— new masks must be given "speech lessons". A mask acquires a repertoire of gestures, props and postures as it develops its personality. Like any other growing person, masks can be playful, aggressive or obscene, often behaving in ways that are very much "out of character" for the mask's user. This can become a powerful way of "meeting your own demons", and realising that not all the behavior we are capable of is in keeping with the way we like to think of ourselves.

Masks can lead rituals, representing an invoked spirit or "leader" of "the sabbat". Groups of masks can develop their own myths, and perform rituals for an unmasked audience. Masks can also be used as "guardians" at a ritual site or temple, and if placed on stands turned inwards towards the ritual, they can seem to be "participating". It is common for "guardian" masks to "call out" to ritual participants that they want to "join in".

PRINCIPLES OF MASK-WORK

There are two basic types of Masks: Full-Face and Half-Face Masks. Full-face masks do not have a mouth, and so cannot speak, relying on physical language to communicate. On the other hand, once Half-face masks learn to speak, they hardly ever stop talking!

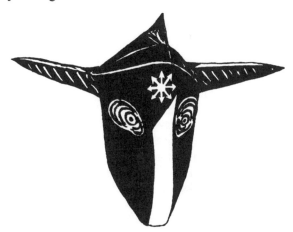

Mask-work cannot be done "cold". It should always be directed by a leader who acts both as an anchor, should people fear that the experience is becoming too much for them, and who can let participants feel comfortable enough to "let go" and allow the mask to take over.

The following exercises can be used as preludes to mask-work:

Animals

This is a game where group members take on animal roles and act them out, with appropriate noises and gestures. It tends to give rise to very stereotyped behavior, such as mock fighting or grooming, but occasionally people do get very "caught-up" in their animal roles, and as such, can be used as a prelude to exploring shape-shifting.

Faces

As we grow up, we tend to adopt characteristic facial expressions—they help establish the sense of personality. These "faces" become etched into our muscle patterns so that they effectively act as "masks" themselves—of fear, pride, anger or resignation. "Faces" begins by all participating making a word-less, emotional noise, then making and holding the face that is appropriate to this noise. The group then mills about for a few minutes, before stopping and exchanging feedback about how people found the exercise. One of the very observable effects of invocation is that often, a person who is invoking upon himself, or alternatively, having another person invoke an entity *into* him, will be seen to undergo marked facial changes. This can be taken as a positive indicator that the subject is becoming, momentarily, someone 'other' than his everyday persona.

Face-Painting

Face-painting can be a useful preparation to working with masks. Some quite startling effects can be created with practice and even subtly applied paint can have a dramatic effect in enhancing an invocation. The application of face make-up has been in itself a ritualised act from the most ancient times—as a way of invoking and projecting an image that one wishes to identify with. It can be extended to body-painting, for example, and used to enhance the animals exercise mentioned earlier. The possibilities are limitless, once you start to explore the different media.

Props

It can be surprising how effective using a simple prop can be as an aid to playing other roles and projecting different images of yourself. An exercise used in a Mask Exploration group was for one person to give everyone else in the group a single prop, and ask them to use it in such a way as to suggest a particular character or stereotype. This was both amusing and instructive. For example, a faded poncho gave rise to Clint Eastwood, complete with slow, purposeful walk and gunfighter's poise. A pair of mirror-shades threw up a Mr. Cool character as you might see in any American cop-show. A shabby overcoat brought out a wheezing tramp. These *characters* were displayed through participants altering their bodily posture, movements, voice and manner. It is quite easy to make yourself into other characters this way, and the skill of doing so can be put to good use in magic. Not only is it a useful exercise in overcoming habitual patterns, but it allows one to be more flexible in assuming different personalities in both group and solo events.

In mask-work, rather than trying to think yourself into the role of the mask, as might be suggested by its appearance, a trick is to stop thinking, and let the mask do the work. The masks personality may arise from the Deep Mind, while the waking awareness is distracted. This can be done by humming loudly to block thoughts while donning the mask.

PRECAUTIONS

Mask-work needs to be approached carefully if it is to be done at all. It is a powerful aspect of dramatic experience and should be respected as such. Some form of Banishing ritual can be a useful method of bringing group sessions to a close.

SOLO WORK

Most of the foregoing has been written from the stance of group workings, but masks can also be used in solo meditation and ritual. Usually, the degree of mask-trance is not as intense as the group-generated effect, but nonetheless it can still be a powerful experience. The most obvious use of masks in solo work is as an aid to invocation made to a particular entity or force. The use of a full-face mask for example, tends to affect the way one moves—the head has to tilt slightly upwards to balance the added weight, and it draws ones attention away from the rest of the body. Also, the ritualised donning of the mask as part of the event can heighten awareness of the sacred nature of the experience. The mask becomes a sacred object, recalling the feelings, images and symbols associated with a particular ritual or event.

Invocation, like other techniques of magic, works through building up chains of association. The use of incense, oils and perfumes, food and drink, colours and clothing are also worthy of consideration.

SMELLS

Smell is probably the least understood and most undervalued of our senses. We rely so much on sight and hearing that smell affects us almost subliminally. This is in contrast to most other animal species. Many animals receive much more information about their environment via smell than sight or sound. The power of smell is that it evokes associations—memories, hunger, sexual arousal and fear, can all be brought into conscious awareness by a particular smell, in a way that is both immediate and intense.

Hence the use of incense in building a ritual atmosphere. Over the last decade or so, the investigation of the properties of smell has increased. Aromatherapy is becoming increasingly popular, and most hospitals now have 'coma kits' which contain very strong synthetic smells which are used to stimulate patients who are in deep coma following a trauma. One of the difficulties with smells is that, unless you are used to working with them, they are difficult to describe. It is much easier to recall a sight than a smell, and when trying to describe a smell from memory, we rely heavily on symbolic associations. This may be due to the fact that, in humans, only a small region of the Thalamus (the area of the brain dealing with sensory information) is concerned with smell. Women are more sensitive to certain smells than men; for example the menstrual cycles of women who live together often become synchronised. This appears to be facilitated by the secretion of pheromones (external chemical messengers). The offering of incense and fragrant perfumes to deities is one of the most ancient forms of worship and invocation. The question of what is the most appropriate form of incense or perfume for a deity is very much a matter of personal choice, and there are basically three approaches to choosing scents. Firstly, there is the way of historical authenticity. Secondly there is the path of magical correspondences, whereby some 'authority' has already decided what smell corresponds to which god, planet, colour, etc. Thirdly, there is the Tao of choosing whatever scent you decide is most appropriate. Some scents do have distinct physiological side-effects, such as clearing the nasal passages or raising skin temperature. Others may be artificial, but no less evocative— there is nothing like the smell of a dentist's waiting room to arouse apprehension and tension for some people, and if you can use such a combination to help build an appropriate ambiance, then by all means use it.

FOOD AND DRINK

Food and drink are often used as sacraments, allowing participants to absorb the divine essence of the invoked entity, and what kinds of food and drink are used can depend very much on the overall ambiance of the ritual. Mead, for example, is the chosen quaff of the Northern (Germanic) Tradition, while some of the Loa of Voudoun are partial to a tot of rum. In Dionysian ritual, the very act of drinking may itself be considered an act of invocation, where the spirit of Dionysus would make himself present in the first celebrant to reach an appropriate state of consciousness. Eating and drinking are themselves sacred acts. Offerings of food made to the gods during ritual is often consumed as part of the general grounding from the working. Moving from 'serious' magical work to feasting and revels is a time-honoured way of closing a ceremony.

CLOTHING

A robe (usually hooded) is considered the basic uniform of the working magician. The robe serves to conceal one's body outline and provide a further level of reinforcement that one is doing something 'different' to acts performed with normal clothes. For most magicians, it seems to be the case that one either works robed, or naked (skyclad). Working naked has its own effects—especially in groups, where newcomers may well experience hang-ups about their own body-image, or harbour the suspicion (usually unfounded) that a group who works naked is going to end up in bed together. Working naked also leads to perceptual changes—the area of skin exposed makes the body surface a more effective sensory organ, and the fact of being naked usually ensures that one is more alert to possible dangers.

DRESSING THE PART

In addition to these basic approaches to clothing, you can also consider 'dressing up' for invocatory ritual. While most magicians tend to make do with visualising themselves wearing the appropriate garb for invoking a particular deity, you can have a lot of fun and achieve some stunning effects by using costumes, masks, face paints, etc., the preparation of which can be as rewarding as the ritual itself.

MUSICAL INSTRUMENTS

The use of musical instruments as an aid to invocation, or even as the main form of invocation, again has an ancient lineage. While tape-recorded music can add ambiance to a ritual, there is nothing to beat actually producing sounds yourself. Here are some examples of easily-obtainable instruments.

Whirlers

The Grecian Iynx is basically a small wheel, suspended at the middle of a loop of string. The string is wound up and, as the string unwinds, the wheel spins, making a rushing, humming sound. The Iynx was used to invoke (and banish) deities, drawing them down to possess a celebrant. It is thought that the Thessalian witches used the Iynx to 'draw down the Moon', and it was widely used in rain-making, binding demons and love-magic.

Related to the Iynx is the Bullroarer, which, at its simplest, is a piece of heavy wood with chamfered edges, at least ten inches long, with a thick length of cord attached. When whirled slowly over one's head, it makes a droning noise, and if whirled at speed, a rushing, humming sound. It is an outdoor instrument, and the user should place himself where unwary onlookers are out of danger of being clouted!

Rhythm-Makers

The use of drums, shakers or handclaps to create rhythms is the simplest and often the most effective enhancement to ritual invocation, particularly in neo-shamanic styles of magic. Drumming itself can sweep a ritual celebrant into possession by a spirit. In the pseudo-Masonic ritual style of post-Golden Dawn magic, handclaps or strikes upon a bell or gong are often used to punctuate different stages of ritual.

Sustained Notes

The singing bell of Tibet is basically a bell with a handle. You hold the handle and rub the bell with a round block of wood very quickly, producing a prolonged singing tone. Lightly tapping a gong with a soft hammer will also produce sustained notes. Also in this category fall breath-powered instruments such as didgeri-doos, bugles, whistles, conches and thighbone trumpets.

CHAPTER NINE

CONQUERING DEMONS

PERSONAL DEMONS

Personal demons are latent structures within the psyche, unresolved complexes and repressed 'voices' thrown up by the ego as a defensive measure. They act seemingly independently of our conscious volition so that we experience them as beyond our control. These structures are habitual emotional or behavioral patterns which are experienced, at times, as problematic—something which has not been successfully integrated, possibly because it has resisted examination or analysis, or through lack of awareness of a habit or pattern, or indeed, how to deal with it. In Tantric practice these 'demons' are known as Kleshas—and the process of working with them is known as Klesha-Smashing.

In a broad sense then, Demons are blocks of behavior—emotional and cognitive responses to life situations. To give an example, Jealousy: in this context, Jealousy is less some tentacled monster that arrives suddenly from another dimension, but rather a response to a situation—you come out of a workshop and have a row with your partner because it seems to you they've been responding to the speakers' flirtatious behavior. Personal demons are summoned into stressful situations. If jealousy is an issue for you, then when you are presented with the evidence which confirms and supports your fears about this issue, out pops the Jealousy Demon in a flurry of accusations and emotional storms.

Unlike the traditional demons from the Grimoires, Personal demons often do not have a shape, sigil, or name, yet they can exert tremendous power over us. And, like the more traditional demons, they can be identified, bound, and, through magical procedures, transformed into something which works *for* us, rather than *against* us. This is where 'Conquering' comes in.

It can be useful to identify these intrapsychic structures as 'demons' for the purposes of working with and integrating them. If you find however, that you are using the idea of having a 'demon' as an excuse for behavior for which you are loath to take responsibility, then you have gone seriously astray. Saying "Oh dear, my Jealousy Demon slipped out which is why I had a temper tantrum when you spoke to so-and-so" is not the most effective way of dealing with Personal Demons: you are admitting that the demon has more control of you than you do of it.

Rather, by isolating the tangle of inner conversations, attitudes, fears, reflexes and fantasies; giving this tangle a distinctive name, shape and sigil, it becomes progressively easier to observe the circumstances in which the demon appears. This involves awareness of the relationship between your own feelings, other people's responses, and how *you* perceive those responses, contribute to feeding the demon power. The fact that these demons appear in everyday situations rather than the isolated conditions of a magical ritual, often makes them harder to deal with.

As Aleister Crowley once said, it's easy for us to summon demons. So make yourself comfortable, and bring into your mind a situation which invokes a demon that you find difficult to subdue. It needn't be anything monumental—any situation which provokes a response which you would like to deal with in a different way.

You will notice that stressful situations often provoke these demons to rise up within us. The fight/flight response kicks in as does depression, fear, anger, etc. All are emotional/cognitive patterns which arise from a condition of physical stimulation—a bodily gnosis, if you like. There is a feedback loop between the physical sensation and the context which kicks off the emotional/ mental response. This gives the first clue for transforming demons from an overwhelming, uncontrollable experience into something which you can understand and bind to your will. Such demons are often related to knots of tension in the body, knots which are drawn ever tighter with each appearance of the demon.

So the first stage is to short-circuit the feedback loop between physical anxiety and the mental and emotional responses.

EMOTIONAL ENGINEERING

Visualise yourself in a situation where one of your personal demons is evoked. Make it as much a worst-case scenario as possible, while remaining aware of how your body feels as memories, fantasies, "what if's" and "what happens when's" whirl you into physiological arousal. You interpret that arousal as something—anger, anxiety, depression, jealousy, possessiveness—which becomes the basis of your awareness and perception. To begin emotional engineering, don't identify the physiological feelings as one thing or another—just experience them as an 'odd' sensation which you cannot define. For example, that nagging sensation which you have come to identify with the desire to smoke a cigarette is merely an 'odd' sensation, the source of which you are not sure of. This process is simple:

1) When you find yourself gripped by a powerful emotion, do not attempt to suppress it, but allow yourself to fully experience it.

2) Be aware of physical sensations as the emotion intensifies.

3) Still your inner dialogue's generation of fantasies, or tendency to drag memories out of the past, which serve to perpetuate and intensify the state.

4) Be aware of bodily sensation alone, and still all cognitive attempts to identify this sensation as one emotion or another.

This leads towards a state of Free Emotion, which could, for instance, be redefined as pleasure or ecstasy. This technique can be used generally in Ego Magic, but is particularly useful for denying power to Personal Demons.

Further clues for working with Personal Demons comes from understanding the different layers which make them up. Demons are not merely physiological identifications, but also behavioral and cognitive. This can be seen when we look at an addiction such as smoking. All excuses about having a cigarette for the special reason of... are inspired by the demon, as are behaviors that maintain the addiction and rationalisations about why we need to maintain the habit. Not only are such Demons contextual, they also *collude* with each other to ensure each other's survival. A person who is having difficulty resisting alcohol might offer a drink to someone who has had a history of such problems. This is not just mutual support; it generates a tacit understanding shared by both, and excludes non-alcoholics as they "don't really understand."

Similarly, a "Jealousy" Demon in one person can collude with a "Fear-of-Restriction" Demon in his partner, sparking a tug-o-war where both demons become stronger, each seemingly defending its own ego-territory, but both committed to surviving and growing.

GANESHA—BINDER OF DEMONS

Ganesha is one of the most popular deities of the Indian subcontinent. Prayers to Ganesha precede all other acts of worship and ceremony. He is invoked to remove obstacles from one's path and to pass luck, he grants prosperity to those who deal in commerce, and freedom to those who seek liberation. Ganesha: vermilion coloured, with the head of an elephant; the body of a man. In his four hands he holds a tusk, a noose, a goad, and makes the gesture of granting boons. He holds in his trunk a pomegranate and the crescent moon is upon his forehead. A serpent is entwined around his split belly. He has the strength of an elephant, the intelligence of man, and the subtlety and cunning of a mouse, which is his vehicle.

The *Upa Parana* details eight incarnations of Ganesha, who fought and overcame obsessional demons: Kaamaasura (lust), Krodhaasura (unjust anger), Lobhaasura (greed), Mohaasura (infatuation), Maatsara (jealousy), Mamaasura (attachment), and Abhimaansura (egotistic pride). Ganesha is often depicted as dancing, for he is playful and filled with joy and delight. Although he subdues demons, he lacks gravity and pride. The son of Shiva and Parvati, he is the beloved one of all the Gods, a very Puckish figure respected by all. Place Ganesha in your belly, and meditate upon his ecstatic dance, for he is freedom personified. He grants wealth, but he is free of attachment to wealth. He is wise, yet not ponderous. He has many talents, yet he is not fettered by them. In most parts of India, he is considered to be celibate, although some Tantric icons of the god show him seated with a Shakti (power). In the aspect of Lakshmi Ganapati (the giver of success) he is flanked by the goddesses Siddhi (achievement) and Buddhi (wisdom). In one of his most popular contemporary forms he holds a noose, an elephant goad, a vessel of sweets, and gives a protective gesture.

There is a rich variety of symbolism contained within the figure of Ganesha. His huge, pot-bellied body represents the Universe—Nature, mankind, and the gods themselves reside within his belly. His elephant's head represents the qualities of the elephant—thus he is affectionate, wise, gentle, and loyal; yet when aroused, he can be extremely ruthless and destructive. His large ears 'like winnowing baskets', sift truth from fiction, and recall the Vedic axiom that learning can only take place by listening at the feet of the Guru. A Tantric interpretation of this idea is that liberation can only be achieved by *paying attention* to what is around you—by stilling the chatter of the internal dialogue and experiencing the world as it is, rather than how you think it is. Ganesha's trunk is symbolic of the quality of discrimination—the first great lesson for any would-be magician. The elephant can use its trunk for heavy tasks, such as moving a log, or very delicate acts. The curved trunk also symbolises the root mantra OM, the sound from which the universe was created. The broken tusk has many associations. It shows, for one thing, that Ganesha is not bound by the desires for balance and symmetry (which are central obsessions in Hindu philosophy). By breaking off a tusk to use as a weapon or pen, Ganesha demonstrates the sacrifice of deities to humanity.

One of the most common 'vehicles' (mounts) associated with Ganesha is the mouse. This is a strange relationship, as, unlike other vehicles, such as the Garuda bird on which Shiva rides, the mouse is never venerated in its own right. This may hearken back to Ganesha's aspect of a harvest deity, when he was propitiated to destroy rodents that threatened crops. The mouse is often associated with small desires and doubts—the kleshas which we continually assail ourselves with. The mouse may also represent cunning, and the ability to achieve desire in non-obvious ways.

GANESHA DEMON-MORPHING

Place yourself in a comfortable position, perform any preferred relaxation exercise, and give attention to your bodily sensations. Close your eyes and turn your mind inwards, towards your belly. Feel that part of your body to be a void, filled with red mist. As you breathe in and out, imagine the form of elephant-headed Ganesha taking shape within your belly. Repeat internally the mantra "Om Ganapati Namah."

Once Ganesha has formed inside you, imagine that you are becoming yourself an image of Ganesha—your nose lengthens to become a trunk, your ears become those of an elephant—feel your body outline changing. When this metamorphosis is complete, turn your attention once again inwards, and then visualise a situation which stirs the evocation of a demon within yourself. See the situation occurring within your belly and see yourself there in it. Be aware of body sensations, but still any thoughts and identifications that arise. Let your breathing become slow and deep, and be aware of how your body feels as pure sensation, without an identification or label.

Slowly, feel that physical sensation to be one of pleasure—a growing sense of joyfulness which you can relax into. Feel that sensation as a source of power, and allow that power to build up inside you until, finally, you have to give voice to it. Repeat the sound that issues from you. A word or mantra may form. If it does, keep hold of it in your mind. At this point, begin the so-called 'Elephant Dance' which is named from the habit of elephants moving their heads from side to side at a watering-hole. Allow your head to loll from side to side, keeping your neck-muscles loose, and move your torso left and right. This movement prevents residual tension settling into the body following the catharsis of the above exercise.

This exercise is useful for Demon work in two ways. Firstly, you can use it to free yourself from the grip of a demonic response that continues long after the initial trigger-event has passed. Secondly, by mentally projecting a situation where a demon might arise, you are learning to identify the characteristic thoughts, feelings, and behavior appropriate to that demon, and so become aware of when you are allowing its responses to carry you away. Once you know the points of the feedback loops, it is easier to break out of them.

It is useful, for this kind of work, that Ganesha is very much a Playful God as it seems to be most effective to approach most kinds of Ego magic from a condition of Playful Relaxation than Grim Determination.

STOP-LOOK-RELAX WORD

Again, visualise a situation that provokes a Demon but this time, let the thoughts, feelings and images whirl around inside your mind—project the appropriate fantasies which give the demon power—let it run away with you. As the feelings churn within your bodymind, see an image taking shape before you—the huge shape of Ganesha towering above you. His eyes twinkle with humour—he lifts his trunk and blasts the air with a ear-splitting trumpet which rips apart the images and thoughts filling your mind—the sound of the trumpet vibrates through your body, until it becomes a sound that you can hear, a sound that you can make, and it wells through you, up into your throat, and out of your mouth. Repeat the sound until it becomes clear for you.

This sound can be used as a STOP-LOOK-RELAX word. The idea is that each time you feel a demon rising within you, hurl the sound at it—to stop it in its tracks, and to stop you feeding it power through fantasy and other reactions. If you can stop yourself from feeding a demon, and relax in its presence, then you are halfway to getting it to work for you in other ways. Demons maintain themselves against discovery and dissolution. If you hurl a word of power at a demon, and relax, viewing the situation calmly and clearly, then you are in a position analogous to Ganesha and the Mouse. At this point you may consider entering into dialogue with the demon—and they have a similar nature to a Russian Doll—a demon which at first seems fearsome, can be stripped away in layers, as you work with it, understanding what part it plays in maintaining you as you 'are' (rather than what you could be). It might be possible to work with it in another way than that which you have been used to.

MAGICAL RESPONSES
1. Feed To Exhaustion

It can sometimes be useful to feed Personal Demons to exhaustion. Often demons retain their power to holding us back from investigating the entire consequences of the fears they stir within us. I recall a possession by my demon of jealousy—instead of suppressing that jealousy or turning it inwards into fear, I let it rage through me, taking every possible manifestation, generating mad plans for revenge and retribution to absurd lengths. In time I was exhausted and found that suddenly, the initial trigger for this possession wasn't important any more—in fact it was laughable.

2. Offer It Death

Personal Demons may occasionally be surprised into immobility if you offer them death—"If...is with someone else, I'm going to kill myself!"—and then you reach out for the razor or samurai sword. Suddenly placing yourself in a situation where the threat of real death is present places everything else in context. Remember, Demons do not want to die, and if you offer them death (and mean it) they are likely to freeze, allowing you to examine them closely.

3. Demonic Pacts

In the common folklore of the occult, there are strict warnings about the 'danger' of Pacts with Demons, as anything remotely 'demonic' belongs to the Lower (base) Self, rather than the Higher (Spiritual) Self, and consequently should be banished. This is equivalent to the Victorians insisting that women keep their ankles covered, lest they inflame the passions of men. If you repress a demon, it becomes all the more powerful and beyond your control. Making a Pact with it, however, implies some kind of tacit understanding between you and the entity. Demons are powerful sources of 'energy'—certainly they are too potentially useful to be banished (suppressed) or given free rein to pull us this way and that.

To enter into a Pact with a Demon, it is first necessary to expose it—to identify its components, sensations, thoughts, behavior; to relate to muscular tension, and even to treat it as a shape, a personality, and give it a magical name and sigil. By deliberately reliving a situation where that demon has overwhelmed you, you learn to understand the points of your relationship to the demon, and how much of that relationship is reciprocal. Such realisations are rarely pleasant, as they involve acknowledging your responsibility for the demon in the first place.

The simplest form of such a Pact is to acknowledge the presence of a demon and transform its action into something which enhances the free expression of your power, rather than hindering it. An example of this process is the transformation of anger into creativity. If someone really annoys me, I am very much tempted to return retribution in the form of a curse. Now to be effective in satisfying this desire for retribution, this curse has to be particularly horrible and devious. Any old "off-the-peg" curse will not suffice. So I begin to start thinking up something really ingenious and unique. What happens is that the desire for individual retribution is supplanted by the desire to create something interesting and new. When I hit upon something which, for me, is a novel perspective on magic (such as the viral Servitors described in Chapter Six), the original 'trigger'—here, the anger and desire to curse the person who triggered that anger—is forgotten. Instead, I focus attention on the new idea, how to integrate it within my existing magical theories-in-use, how to try it out and its wider applications beyond mere cursing. It is a mistake, although a tempting one, to label 'negative' emotional responses as demonic. Your anger in a situation may be perfectly legitimate—it's the way that you express that anger that is important. For example, you could consider your tendency to suppress growing anger until you have an uncontrolled outburst as dysfunctional, and work upon it accordingly. Redirecting and channeling the power of a demon is satisfying— as both of you are working together. At one office where I worked, one of the secretaries seemed to be particularly good at annoying me, making what I found to be asinine comments at the least appropriate moments. This tended to lead to a situation where I suppressed my annoyance until I shouted at her, whereupon she became defensive and shouted back—a situation which quickly escalated beyond the point of sanity. One morning however, as soon as she began her tirade of remarks during a complex and intricate repair job, I took a deep breath and said "Mary, if you don't shut up I'm going to bang your head against your computer monitor"—in a very calm, quiet, and measured voice. "That's not very nice" she replied, whereupon I said "It's not meant to be. This is a difficult job that I'm doing and you are annoying me." The result was that she shut up, and I was able to acknowledge my anger forcefully, convey my feelings to her clearly, without becoming tense or carrying that anger around with me for the next hour or so, making my job all the more difficult.

4. Banishing With Extreme Prejudice

While it is necessary to identify, know and integrate your own Personal Demons, it is arguable how far you can take this process with other people. It may occur, for example, that a friend or lover is clearly harbouring dysfunctional demons, be they Ego demons such as Jealousy or Possessiveness patterns, to more physiological demons such as alcoholism, drug addiction, or pathological violence. If someone you are having a relationship with is clearly subject to the will of a demon, such as an alcohol or Heroin Demon, then despite all protests to the contrary, that demon has a potentially greater influence upon them than you ever will. All addiction-demons survive by demonstrating unequivocally to their hosts that their panacea is ultimately more reliable than anything else. When there is an emotional attachment made to another person, it is difficult to have the necessary detachment, objectivity and cruelty to act as an effective therapist/exorcist. Thus the admonition—Banish with Extreme Prejudice. Get them out and keep them out. Powerful demons such as these will do anything possible to draw you into the host's behavior patterns. It can be useful here to separate addict and demon into two entities. Banish the demon if only to make it aware that you are aware of it.

THE PERSONAL GENIUS

The concept of the Personal Genius, the creative source of power and inspiration, has been given many different masks and labels. Healers often say that the power that flows through them is from God or a particular Archangel. Some magicians call this experience the 'Knowledge and Conversation of the Holy Guardian Angel' while some psychotherapists and New Agers talk about contacting the Higher Self. The most useful reference to the experience I have found is in Aleister Crowley's novel, *Moonchild*.

This is analogous to a Tantric exercise called "Feeding the Fire." You imagine that your body is hollow, and that within it is a flickering flame, which feeds on all your experience. Each breath fans the flame, each moment of awareness feeds the flame, all emotions, thoughts, victories, defeats, identifications, revulsions—all feed the flame. All experience becomes the fuel for this inner flame, from which emanates the power to illuminate. The aim of all such exercises is to attain a degree of non-attachment to your actions and works. In Tantric methodology this flame is also Kundalini-Shakti, the organising and creative power that is equally present in humans and stars. Such power is not under the control of the ego, and any tendencies to identify it as belonging exclusively to you will weaken its expression *through* you. A useful attitude to cultivate in this respect is that by removing all tendencies to create identifications and blocks within yourself, you are making yourself into a hollow pipe through which power may flow freely.

CHANNELED ENTITIES

This term covers all types of entities to whom is attributed advanced wisdom and teachings; spirit guides, enlightened masters, space beings, Higher Selves and Guardian Angels. Making contact with such entities may be useful, up to a point. The old saying "it doesn't matter what you say, it's the way you say it" is certainly true of the channeling phenomenon. The message from these cuddly cosmic beings is overwhelmingly one of love and harmony. Love yourself, be yourself. We are all immortal and we can all be healed by using the power of the New Age clichés—rays, chakras, auras, colours, and pseudo-scientific jargon. A welter of impressive terms and meaningless catch-phrases. Platitudinous pap fed to an uncritical audience eager to believe in a cartoon universe where no one really dies, no one really gets hurt, no one really thinks for themselves and I suppose, Napalm doesn't really stick to kids. Rapping with Ramtha will heal you of your mental troubles, and everything will become ginger-peachy.

A funny thing about those higher beings, their message stays the same whenever they appear, but each new wave of popularity gives them a new mailing address. The Spiritualists had their Red Indian guides, the Theosophists tuned into vibes beamed out by Tibetan "Masters". Aleister Crowley claimed to have been in contact with extra-terrestrials, and by the nineteen-fifties the Gods were using flying saucers to get about. Jesus is alive and well and living on Venus! Now it's the day of the dolphin. It's interesting however, that very often, the founts of wisdom appear to be endangered species. Dolphins, Red Indians, and Aborigines have all suffered extensively at the hands of us well-fed White folks. We ripped off the wealth of the Asian subcontinent and then swarmed over there in droves to seek spiritual enlightenment. Maybe behind all this new age bit is the guilt of the overfed trying not to feel impotent while the world changes around them. That's what is so attractive about the channelers' entities. They don't ask us to do anything as unattractive as look at what's happening behind the scenes. No, they wrap reality up in ribbons and glitter so that life becomes a continuously-looping Walt Disney dreamworld.

What seems to be implicit here is that messages from "higher beings" (whatever their alleged source) are automatically benign and helpful. Quite a turnabout from the 'fifties, when the aliens brought to us by Hollywood came down out of the skies to ravage, rape our daughters and take over the world for no very good reason. Maybe they've just changed their act. After all, they should know by now that if they come barging in with death rays blazing we'll just nuke them into radioactive debris. So they've adopted the soft-sell approach—they're going to love us to death, 'till we're smothered under a security blanket of bliss. They've also found a message that is attractive—one that says it's OK to have money, a Porsche, etc., and that spirituality is about loving yourself. Channeled entities will tell you about your wonderful past incarnations in Lemuria or Atlantis, what you did, who your partner was and so forth.

The quality that the Channelers often seem to lack is that of discrimination, which is very necessary whenever one approaches communications between humans and higher entities, whether they be dolphins, deities, extra-terrestrials or intelligent poodles from Sirius B. Magicians who employ the magical techniques of post-Golden Dawn systems tend, in my experience, to approach the whole area of inner-plane contacts with a good deal of healthy skepticism (another quality which seems to be sadly lacking in new age philosophy). Thelemic magicians often test the validity of a contact by pronouncing those fateful words "Do What Thou Wilt Shall be The Whole of The Law," to which the entity makes the suitable rejoinder, or disappears, shrieking, into the nearest astral discontinuity. A similar check involves mentally projecting the seal of the A∴A∴ onto the entity. The cross-examination of entities using symbolism and Gematria is also often resorted. Such methods, together with ritual (or other) techniques help ensure that the beings invoked are who they claim they are. Like most other magicians who go around invoking all manner of 'orrible things (sorry, inner-plane adepts) I've received a wide variety of communications from various entities over the years. These communications are only relevant to me and I'm certainly not going to offer them up as great cosmic insights. What I do demand is that they make sense, if only in terms of what I've been doing recently. Any one can go on about cosmic love, harmony, beauty and heavy karma (...maan) but it's much more instructive when the message is informative, in terms of pointers on how to look at a particular issue, problem, or internally-consistent symbolic messages.

There does seem to be a kind of cumulative degeneration of the quality of such communications. Having read quite a wide variety of such stuff recently, I see a kind of pattern emerging. The initial contact with an entity can produce some quite startling transmissions—in terms of synthesising information in new ways. Then, as the recipient becomes more and more bound up with the communications, they degenerate in terms of quality of information until one is hearing the kind of cosmic mind-mush which, though it sounds good, is rather obvious. It seems that, the more a person identifies (in terms of ego-involvement) with an entity, the less original the topics of communication become. Before long the recipient of such messages begins to hail themselves as Priest/Priestess of the "mysteries" revealed exclusively to them, and the foundation of a small cult that is going to save the world shortly follows.

All of which begs the question of just what is going on when we contact these entities? A difficult one, this. How we try and answer it says more about how we structure meaning than any actual organisation of inner realms. The Channeler-type answer of course is that all these entities are actual, separate beings hanging about around the astral planes (no doubt at a never-ending cocktail party) until they pop down to deliver reassurance to a group of yuppies about heart disease, second mortgages and the Dow-Jones index. An utter skeptic might answer that they are all imaginary and therefore unreal. A magician might answer that while these entities do not have a wholly objective existence, they are not fictitious either. People still tend to speak of the imagination as a source of experience that is somehow less real than everything else. An interesting model for examining inner-plane contacts can be found within William Gibson's novel, *Neuromancer.* One of the major characters is an Artificial Intelligence which manipulates a cast of humans to further its own ends. To successfully do this it must establish a rapport with those it wishes to manipulate. It does this by generating constructs—personalities which it wears like masks, creating them out of the memories of the humans it wishes to contact. It explains that it needs these masks to establish a point of access—

an interface—between its own experience and the perceptual limits of human beings.

Reading this brought very much to mind accounts of human-entity contacts. Particularly a sentence in Dion Fortune's *The Cosmic Doctrine* which reads:

> What we are you cannot realise and it is a waste of time to try and do so but you can imagine (italics mine) us on the astral plane and we can contact you through your imagination, and though your mental picture is not real or actual, the results of it are real and actual.

Dion Fortune made extensive use of inner-plane contacts to synthesise her magical ideas. Alan Richardson, in his biography of Dion Fortune, *Priestess,* discusses the various historical figures that Fortune claimed to be in contact with. The most interesting entity is one "David Carsons", whom according to Fortune, was a young British officer who was killed during the first World War. Fortune provided a good deal of biographical information concerning Carsons, and after thorough research, Alan Richardson states that Carsons did not exist! Rather, it seems, he was actually, in terms of the above model, a construct; a personality generated out of Dion Fortune's experimental magic and experiences, and hence an interface for accessing information.

If you imagine the sum total of your personal memories and knowledge as a sphere in space—the unknown—then to extend your sphere of information it is as though a window must be created, through which the unknown, or raw data, can be translated into information that is meaningful in terms of perceptual limitations. Inner-plane entities are how we tend to conceptualise these windows into chaos. They appear as independent entities so that we can make sense of the incoming data. Their personalities are usually concurrent with the recipient's belief system. Hence the many forms of the entities, depending on where you believe the seat of wisdom is, be it Egypt, Sirius B, or some draughty monastery in Tibet. Usually, it seems, these entities are automatically generated as one focuses will and imagination towards any one vector, but occasionally entities can be generated as an act of will, so that "outposts" can be established within which personal ideas and innerworlds can be explored and eventually integrated into one's psychocosm. At this point the whole issue of the "reality" of the experience breaks down, as these entities are not simply "secondary personalities" in the pathological sense, but constructs which are emergent properties of our information-processing capacity interacting with that which lies beyond it.

So how does this relate to the higher beings contacted by the New Age Channelers? I feel that this is a question of degree. Most magicians I have encountered who make use of innerworld contacts are doing so as part of going beyond the limits of normality; finding an edge and pushing themselves repeatedly over it, sifting for insights in abyss after abyss. On the other hand, the New Age Channelers seem to want nothing more than the spiritual equivalent of a candy-flavoured infant pacifier. It is as though they are channeling not so much information from outside the human knowledge-pool, but very much from within it—the "higher-authority" control programs of a culture in need of a mysticism which embraces materialism and a bland, "I'm OK—so there!" view of the world. Strip away the therapol jargon and the diluted Eastern mysticism, and the New Age consciousness is revealed as just another scam of the Slave-Gods. An escape route that leads nowhere, because it does not involve risking or challenging the ego. Hence its attraction for those who need to follow creeds and gurus. Let's face it, the world can be a pretty daunting place. If some wise adept in the body of a Joan Collins lookalike told you that 'life' on the astral plane was an endless round of Dynasty-style parties, wouldn't you sign up for a course in Astral Projection?

CHAPTER TEN

ARE YOU ILLUMINATED?

Magic is often referred to in terms of being a path, a spiritual quest, a voyage of self-discovery, or an adventure. However you want to dress it up, one point is clear, it is a means of bringing about Change. For this change to be effective, it is important that you be able to set the effects of your magical work within a context—to be able to make sense of them and integrate them into a dynamic interaction with a moving, fluid universe.

This requires a sense (however tenuous) of where you have been, and where you are 'going'. At times these anchor-points will seem to be solid, and at others, ephemeral and faint. Initiation is the term which magicians use to examine this process of integration, and Illumination is one of its most important by-products.

INITIATION AS A PROCESS

There appears to be some misunderstanding over what exactly the term 'initiation' means. Occasionally one bumps into people consider themselves as 'initiates' and seem to consider themselves somehow 'above' the rest of humanity. Particularly irritating are the self-styled 'initiates' who let drop teasing bits of obscure information and then refuse to explain any further because their audience are not 'initiates'. The term itself seems to crop up in a wide variety of contexts—people speak of being 'initiated' into groups, onto a particular path, or of initiating themselves. Some hold that 'initiation' is only valid if the person who confers it is part of a genuine tradition, others that it doesn't matter either way. Dictionary definitions of initiation allude to the act of beginning, or of setting in motion, or entry into something. One way to explain initiation is to say that it is *a threshold of change* which we may experience at different times in our lives, as we grow and develop. The key to initiation is *recognising* that we have reached such a turning point, and are aware of being in a period of transition between our past and our future. The conscious awareness of entering a transitional state allows us to perhaps, discard behavioral/emotional patterns which will be no longer valid for the 'new' circumstances, and consciously take up new ones.

What magical books often fail to emphasise is that initiation is a process. It doesn't just happen once, but can occur many times throughout an individual's life, and that it has peaks (initiatory crises), troughs (black depression or the 'dark night of the soul') and plateaus (where nothing much seems to be going on). becoming aware of your own cycles of change, and how to weather them, is a core part of any developmental process or approach to magical practice. The key elements or stages of the initiation process have been extensively mapped by anthropologists such as Joseph Campbell. While they are mostly used to describe stages of shamanic initiation, they are equally applicable to other areas of life experience.

CRISIS AND CALL

In shamanic societies the first stage of the initiation process is often marked by a period of personal crises and a 'call' towards starting the shamanic journey. Most of us are quite happy to remain within the conceptual and philosophical boundaries of Consensus Reality (the everyday world). For an individual beginning on the initiatory journey, the crisis may come as a powerful vision, dreams, or a deep (and often disturbing) feeling to find out what is beyond the limits of normal life. It can often come as a result of a powerful spiritual, religious or political experience, or as a growing existential discontent with life. Our sense of being a stable self is reinforced by the "walls" of the social world in which we participate—yet our sense of uniqueness resides in the cracks of those same walls. Initiation is a process which takes us "over the wall" into the unexplored territories of the possibilities which we have only half-glimpsed. This first crisis is often an unpleasant experience, as we begin to question and become dissatisfied with all that we have previously held dear—work, relationships, ethical values, family life can all be disrupted as the individual becomes increasingly consumed by the desire to 'journey'.

The internal summons may be consciously quashed or resisted, and it is not unknown for individuals in tribal societies to refuse 'the call' to shamanic training—no small thing, as it may lead to further crises and even death. One very common experience of people who feel the summons in our society is an overpowering sense of urgency to either become 'enlightened' or to change the world in accordance with emerging visions. This can lead to people becoming 'addicted' to spiritual paths, wherein the energy that may have been formerly channeled into work or relationships is directed towards taking up spiritual practices and becoming immersed in 'spiritual' belief systems.

The 'newly awakened' individual can be (unintentionally) as boring and tiresome as anyone who has seized on a messianic belief system, whether it be politics, religion, or spirituality. It is often difficult, at this stage in the cycle, to understand the reaction of family, friends and others who may not be sympathetic to one's new-found direction or changes in lifestyle. Often, some of the more dubious religious cults take advantage of this stage by convincing young converts that "true friends" etc., would not hinder them in taking up their new life, and that anyone who does not approve, is therefore not a 'true friend'.

There are a wide variety of cults which do well in terms of converts from young people who are in a period of transition (such as when leaving home for the first time) and who are attracted to a belief/value system that assuages their uncertainties about the world. Another of the problems often experienced by those feeling the summons to journey is a terrible sense of isolation or alienation from one's fellows—the inevitable result of moving to the edge of one's culture. Thus excitement at the adventure is often tinged with regret and loss of stability or unconscious participation with one's former world. Once you have begun the process of disentanglement from the everyday world, it is hard not to feel a certain nostalgia for the lost former life in which everything was (seemingly) clear-cut and stable, with no ambiguities or uncertainties.

A common response to the summons to departure is the journey into the wilderness—of moving away from one's fellows and the stability of consensual reality. A proto-shaman is likely to physically journey into the wilderness, away from the security of tribal reality, and though this is possible for some Westerners, the constraints of modern living usually mean that for us, this wandering in the waste is enacted on the plane of ideas, values and beliefs, wherein we look deeply within and around ourselves and question everything, perhaps drawing away from social relations as well. Deliberate isolation from one's fellows is a powerful way of loosening the sense of having fixed values and beliefs, and social deprivation mechanisms turn up in a wide variety of magical cultures.

THE INITIATORY SICKNESS

In shamanic cultures, the summons to journey is often heralded by a so-called 'initiatory sickness', which can either come upon an individual suddenly, or creep slowly upon them as a progressive behavioral change. Western observers have labeled this state as a form of 'divine madness', or evidence of psycho-pathology. In the past, anthropologists and psychologists have labeled shamans as schizophrenic, psychotic, or epileptic. More recently, western enthusiasts of shamanism (and anti-psychiatry) have reversed this process of labeling and asserted that people as schizophrenic, psychotic or epileptic are proto-shamans. Current trends in the study of shamanism now recognise the former position to be ethnocentric—that researchers have been judging shamanic behavior by western standards. The onset of initiatory sickness in tribal culture is recognised as a difficult, but potentially useful developmental process. Part of the problem here is that western philosophy has developed the idea of 'ordinary consciousness', of which anything beyond this range is pathological, be it shamanic, mystical, or drug-induced. Fortunately for us, this narrow view is being rapidly undermined.

Individuals undergoing the initiatory sickness do sometimes appear to suffer from fits and 'strange' behavior, but there is an increasing recognition that it is a mistake to sweepingly attach western psychiatric labels onto them (so that they can be explained away). Shamans may go through a period of readjustment, but research shows that they tend to become the most healthy people in their tribes, functioning very well as leaders and healers.

Transitional states showing similar features to the initiatory sickness have been identified in other cultures' mystical and magical practices, which western researchers are beginning to study, as practices from other cultures gain popularity in the west.

THE DARK NIGHT OF THE SOUL

St. John of the Cross, a Christian mystic, wrote of this experience:

> (it)...puts the sensory spiritual appetites to sleep, deadens them, and deprives them of the ability to find pleasure in anything. It binds the imagination, and impedes it from doing any good discursive work. It makes the memory cease, the intellect become dark and unable to understand anything, and hence it causes the will to become arid and constrained, and all the faculties empty and useless. And over this hangs a dense and burdensome cloud, which afflicts the soul, and keeps it withdrawn from God.

When entering the 'Dark Night' one is overcome by the sense of spiritual dryness and depression. The idea, expressed in some quarters, that all such experiences are to be avoided in favour of a peaceful life, shows up the superficiality of so much of contemporary living. The Dark Night is a way of bringing the soul to stillness, so that a deep psychic transformation may take place. In the Western Esoteric Tradition, this experience is reflected in the Tarot card 'The Moon' and is the 'hump' in an individual's spiritual development where any early benefits of meditation, Pathworking or disciplines appear to cease, and there is an urge to abandon such practices and return to 'everyday' life. This kind of 'hump' which must be passed through can be discerned in different areas of experience, and is often experienced by students on degree courses and anybody who is undergoing a new learning process which involves marked life changes as well.

MACRO AND MICRO-INITIATIONS

Generally speaking, there are two kinds of initiatory experience—Microscopic and Macroscopic. Macroscopic initiations can be characterised as being major life shifts, traumas that sweep upon us—the collapse of a long-term relationship, the crash of a business or the sudden knowledge that you have a terminal illness. Such experiences are *global,* which is to say that they send shock waves into every aspect of our lives.

Microscopic initiations are more specific in their actions. One day I was sitting tapping figures into the company accounting program, when I suddenly found myself thinking "I'd like to do an Accounts Course." Now normally I would have regarded that as no more realistic than a wish to fly to the Moon tomorrow. Accounting is one of those tasks I am only too happy to leave up to someone else, and suddenly, I was becoming interested in it! Such new-found interests, particularly in subjects that you have accepted that you dislike or are uninterested in, can be likened to a small flame (symbolised by the Ace of Wands in Tarot) which could easily burn out again if smothered or ignored. The trick is to recognise that you are standing at a crossroads—a threshold of change. This recognition is the key to all initiations. Again, the A PIE formula is of use:

Assess

Stop. Look around you and assess your situation. Examine all possibilities for future action—there will always be more pathways available than is at first immediately obvious. What possible futures can you jump into? Use any technique that will gather useful information—options lists, divination, dream-oracles or asking your favourite deity. Often, all you have to do is open yourself to become vulnerable to the forces of Change.

Plan

Once you have chosen a course of action—plan what you need to do. What resources do you need? These may be material, magical, financial and perhaps most importantly, the support of other people. Be prepared to carry your plan onwards.

Implement

This is the hardest thing of all—to do what must be done. Often, fear will intervene at this stage. Be prepared to look at your motivations for not continuing upon your chosen course. Unacknowledged fears often take the form of inertia and laziness. Each step forwards gives further momentum to the next effort. Each barrier breached releases a rush of pleasure and freedom.

Evaluate

This is the stage of assimilation—not merely the practice of writing up one's magical record, but being able to look back at your course through the initiatory period and realise what happened and how you dealt with it. Have you learned any important lessons? The value of such experience is to make knowledge flesh—assimilating experience until it seems perfectly simple and natural.

GETTING THE FEAR

A key to understanding initiatory states is that they bring with them varying degrees of fear. One of the characteristics of Macroscopic Initiations is that suddenly, our current repertoire of coping strategies are useless. If something into which we have invested a good deal of emotional commitment and self-esteem is directly threatened or removed, and we are placed in a position of being unable to do anything about this, fear is often the dominant emotion.

Fear is the bodily gnosis which reinforces any emotional and cognitive patterns which serve us to hold change at bay. Fear is basically an Excitatory state—the fight/flight reflex of the Autonomic Nervous System firing up. Using the Emotional Engineering techniques described in the previous chapter, you can deconstruct fear into excitement, which can then be used to gather momentum for moving over a threshold into change, rather than reinforcing your own resistance.

RELAX INTO FEAR

This is a process of orienting yourself so that you are sufficiently open to all the different possibilities that each moment of experience offers—enmeshed in the world in an attitude of receptive wonder. This is the knowledge that at any time, without warning, any life event could spin you sideways into Illumination. The sudden-ness of such an experience is one of the underlying themes encapsulated in the Great God Pan. Pan represents creative derangement, the possibility of moving from one state to another, from ordinary perception to divine inspiration. Pan can leap upon you any time, any place with the sudden realisation that everything is alive and significant. In such an experience, physical arousal is a strength, rather than a weakness. Allowing yourself to be vulnerable to the possibility of change means letting into your life wild magic and the power of surprises. Initiatory states often tip us into mental entropy and confusion, and this is a good time to free yourself from the bonds of the Past and the fetters of anticipated futures, and live in the now of your physical presence. Transform fear into wonder and open yourself to new possibilities. Transform fear into fuel and examine the thresholds and personal demons which hinder movement. This state is a form of ecstasy—a word which means "away from stillness," implying some kind of agitation.

SAHAJA

Sahaja is a Sanskrit word which can be translated as 'spontaneity.' If you can learn to relax within initiatory periods, abandoning all set routines and learned responses, you can act with a greater degree of freedom. Periods of initiation can be looked upon as windows of opportunity for major work upon yourself. So what kind of techniques are appropriate here? Anything that enables you to make shifts in your Achievable Reality threshold. Procedures borrowed from NLP, Vivation, Bioenergetics or the various psychotherapies might prove useful here. What you should bear in mind is that recognition that you are entering a threshold of change is all-important. It is difficult to intentionally propel yourself into such states, particularly as at some point during the experience, it is necessary to surrender control.

The initiatory crisis tends to drive home (often very forcefully) the awareness of the fragility of day-to-day experiences, and of the hidden complexity behind that which we have taken for granted as normal. We have become addicted to a 'sameness' of experience, and thus have difficulty coping with novelty or change. Hence the tendency, when faced with a crisis, to rely on learned habits, rather than actually observing the situation. Conversely, the magician has to recognise that there may well be an abyss around every corner, and that what rushes full-tilt at us must be faced head-on. In time, you will come to recognise that you have your own personal cycles of initiation—peaks, troughs and plateaus; you may well come to recognise that you are about to enter an initiatory period, and brace yourself accordingly.

INNERWORLD CONFRONTATIONS

Many world myths feature the descent into the Underworld as a central theme for transformation and the quest for power and mastery of self. The recognition of the necessity of 'rites of passage' is played out both in tribal societies where the death of childhood and the rebirth into adulthood is marked by a rite of passing, and in Western magical and religious societies where 'followers' are reborn into a new selfdom. Death by dismemberment is a strongly recurrent theme in shamanic cultures, where proto-shamans are stripped of their flesh and torn apart by spirits, only to be remade anew, usually with some additional part, such as an extra bone, organ, or crystal as an indication that they are now something 'more' than previously. In some cultures (such as in the Tibetan Tantric Chod ritual), the dismemberment experience is a voluntary meditation, whereas in others, it is an involuntary (though understood) experience.

This kind of transition is not uncommon in Western approaches to magical development, both as a willed technique and as a (seemingly) spontaneous experience that results from working within a particular belief-system. I have for example, been burnt alive in the pyre of Kali, and more recently, had an eye ripped out by the Morrigan. Periodic descents into the Underworld are a necessary phase in the cycle of personal development, and is also associated with depth psychotherapy. According to the Western Esoteric Tradition, one of the key stages of initiatory confrontation is the encounter with 'The Dweller on the Threshold'. Less prosaically, this phrase refers to the experience of our understanding of the gulf between the ego's fiction of itself and our selves as we truly are. This necessitates the acceptance of light into the dark corners of the self, and the acceptance of our short-comings, blind spots and personal weaknesses as aspects of ourselves that we must take responsibility for. The recognition that we are, ultimately, responsible for all aspects of ourselves, especially those bits which we are loath to admit to ourselves, is a step that must be taken if the initiatory journey is to proceed. It is not uncommon for people to remain at this stage for years, or to come back to it, time and time again. Such ordeals must be worked through, or they will return to 'haunt' us until they are tackled, else they will become 'obsessional complexes' (demons) that will grow until they have power over us. There are a myriad of techniques— both magical exercises and psychotherapeutic tools which can be actively used to examine these complexes, but the core of this ordeal is the beginnings of seeing yourself. In shamanic cultures, physical isolation from the tribe is often reinforced by physical ordeals such as fasting, sleep deprivation, and exposure to rigours of heat or cold—all powerful techniques for producing altered states of consciousness.

The initiatory cycle can be likened to a snake sloughing off its skin. So too, we must be prepared to slough off old patterns of thought, belief (about ourselves and the world) and behavior that are no longer appropriate for the new phase of our development. As we reach the initiatory stage of descent into the underworld, so we are descending into the Deep Mind, learning to rely on our own intuition about what is right for us, rather than what we have been told is correct. As the initiatory process becomes more and more intense, we reach a point where we have (to varying degrees) isolated ourselves from the Social World, (physically or mentally), and begun to dismember the layer of our Personal World, so that the Mythic World becomes paramount in our consciousness, perhaps in an intensely 'real' way that it has not been, beforehand. When we open up the floodgates of the Mythic World, we may find that our Deep Mind 'speaks' to us using what psychologists call 'autosymbolic images'; that is, symbols which reflect the churnings within us. These may well be entities or spirits from magical or religious belief systems that we have consciously assimilated, or they may arise 'spontaneously' from the Deep Mind. These 'entities' (whatever their source) may become the first of our 'allies' or guides through the inner worlds that we have descended into. Accounts of shamanic initiation often recount the neo-shaman being 'tested' in various ways by spirit guides and helpers, and, if she or he pass the testing, they become allies that the shaman can call upon, on returning from the underworld. Not all of the spirits one meets while undergoing the underworld experience will be helpful or benign; some will try to mislead or misdirect you. In this kind of instance you will need to rely even more on your own 'truthsense' or discrimination. Ghosts are notoriously capricious, and an 'elder brother' once told me to 'be wary of spirits which herald a false dawn under the dark moon'. Particular 'misguides' to watch out for are the spirits who will tell you that you are 'mystically illuminated' beyond a point that anyone else has reached—they are 'parts' of the ego attempting to save itself from destruction. You may have to 'overcome' some of these spirits—not so much by defeating them in astral combat, but by recognising that they have no power over you— that you understand their seductions and will not be swayed by them. The danger here hearkens back to the necessity of attempting to shed light on as many of your buried complexes as possible—'misguide' spirits will attempt to seduce you into feeding those complexes so that you become caught up in them. Spirit guides and helpers usually come in a variety of forms and shapes. Their messages may not always be obvious, and may only become clear with hindsight—but then you cannot expect everything to be handed to you on a plate. It is not unknown for spirit guides to put the initiate through a pretty rough time, again to test their 'strength', as it were. Powerful spirits don't tend to 'like' shamans who won't take chances or face difficulties and overcome them. This is a hard time to get through, but if you keep your wits about you and hang on in there, then the rewards are worth it. Guides will often show you 'secret routes' through the underworld, and 'places of power' there which you can access at a later point. Some Amerind shamanic traditions involve the shaman descending into the underworld periodically to learn the names of spirits which, when brought out again, can be placed in masks or other ritual objects.

Another benefit of the 'ordeals' stage is Inderworld Mapping—obtaining (or verifying) a symbolic plan of the connecting worlds that form the universe. Western occulture gives us conscious access to a wide variety of universal route maps, the Tree of Life that appears in many esoteric systems being just one well-known example. Western-derived maps seem to have a tendency to become very complicated very quickly— perhaps this reflects a cultural tendency to try and label everything neatly away. The interesting (and intriguing) thing about using innerworld maps is that you can metaprogram your Deep Mind to accept a number of different maps—images and symbols will arise accordingly. Our 'tradition' for receiving innerworld maps (and indeed, any other esoteric teaching) is largely through the written word, rather than oral teaching or the psychoactively-inspired communion with the tribal meme-pool which are the most common routes for shamans. But it is worth remembering that all the different innerworld maps had to come from somewhere, and the most likely source would seem to be the initiatory ordeals of very early shamans, which eventually became condensed into definite structures.

ILLUMINATION

The 'peak' of the initiation experience is that of death/rebirth, and subsequent 'illumination'. That such an experience is common to all mystery religions, magical systems and many secular movements indicates that it may well be one of the essential manifestations of the process of change within the human psyche. Illumination is the much-desired goal for which many thousands of people worldwide, have employed different psycho-technologies, and developed their own psychocosms. Illumination has also been linked with the use of LSD and similar drugs, and perhaps most mysteriously of all, it can occur seemingly spontaneously, to people who have no knowledge or expectation of it. What characterises an experience of illumination? Some of the prevalent factors are:

1. A sense of unity—a fading of the self-other divide
2. Transcendence of space and time as barriers to experience
3. Positive sensations
4. A sense of the numinous
5. A sense of certitude—the "realness" of the experience
6. Paradoxical insights
7. Transience—the experience does not last
8. Resultant change in attitude and behavior.

In neurological terms such experiences represent a re-organising of activity in the brain as a whole. The loss of ego boundary and the involvement of all senses suggests that the Reticular Formation is being influenced so that the processes which normally convey a sense of being rooted in space-time are

momentarily inhibited. The "floating" sensation often associated
with astral projection and other such phenomena suggests that
the Limbic system of the brain stem (which processes
proprioceptive information about the body's location in space) is
also acting in an unusual mode.

What are the fruits of this experience—the insights,
perceptions and messages brought back down to earth by the
illuminate? Evolution of consciousness, by such means, could
well be an important survival program—a way of going beyond
the information given—a way of learning how to modify the
human biosystem via the environment. Ilya Prigognine's theory
of "dissipative structures" shows how the very instability of open
systems allows them to be self-transforming. The basis of this
idea is that the movement of energy through a system causes
fluctuations which, if they reach a critical level (i.e., a
catastrophe cusp point) develop novel interactions until a new
whole is produced. The system then reorganises itself into a new
"higher order" which is more integrated than the previous
system, requires a greater amount of energy to maintain itself,
and is further disposed to future transformation. This can equally
apply to neurological evolution, using a psycho-technology
(ancient or modern) as the tool for change. The core stages of the
process appear to be:

1. Change
2. Crisis
3. Transcendence
4. Transformation
5. Predisposition to further change.

Also, the term 'illumination' is itself, significant. Visions of
light that suddenly burst forth upon the individual are well-
documented from a wide variety of sources, from shamanic
travelers to St. Paul; acid trippers to people who seemingly have
the experience spontaneously. Similarly, the experience of being
'born-again' is central to shamanism, religions and magical
systems. One's old self dies, and a new one is reborn from the
shattered patterns and perceptions. This is well understood in
cultures where there is a single predominant Mythic reality.
Death-rebirth is the key to shamanic development, and many
shamanic cultures interpret the experience quite literally, rather

than metaphorically. Western psychologists are only just beginning to understand the benefits of such an experience. What is clear, is that for many people who undergo it, the experience is unsettling and disturbing, especially when there is no dominant cultural backdrop with which to explain or understand the process. A good example to look at (which always raises hackles in some quarters) is the LSD death-rebirth experience. Some western 'authorities' on spiritual practice hold that drug-induced experiences are somehow not as valid as ones triggered by 'spiritual' practices. Fortunately, this somewhat blinkered view is receding as more information about the role played by psychoactive substances in shamanic training is brought to light. The positive benefits of LSD have been widely proclaimed by people as diverse as Aldous Huxley, Timothy Leary, and Stanislav Grof, all of whom also stressed that acid should be used in 'controlled conditions', rather than, as is so often the case today, indiscriminately. What must be borne in mind about LSD (like other psychoactives) is that its action and effects are highly dependent upon individual beliefs and expectations, and social conditioning. Dropping acid can lead to lasting change and transformation in a positive sense; equally, it can lead to individuals uncritically accepting a set of beliefs and patterns that effectively wall them off from further transformations—witness the number of burnt-out acidheads who become 'Born-Again' evangelicals, for instance. It's not so much the experience itself, but how individuals assimilate it in terms of cultural expectations.

As an example of how this process operates, contrast a proto-shaman against a member of a postmodern, industrial culture such as is our own. The proto-shaman undergoes death-rebirth, and, following illumination, is reborn into the role of a practising shaman, with all its subsequent status affiliations and expectations. Would that it were as simple for Westerners! Ours is a much more complex set of social relations than the tribal environment. Though one might be tempted to think of oneself as a shaman-in-the-making, it's a safe bet that not everyone else is going to accede that role to you. It's tempting, and entirely understandable to think: "Right, that's it. I'm 'illuminated' now—I've been there, done it, etc." and sit back on one's laurels, as it were. While for some of us, one death-rebirth experience alone is enough to jolt us into a new stage of development, it's more often the case that what we do afterwards is critically important. Zero states of having 'made it' are very seductive, but our conditioning patterns are insidious—creeping back into the psyche while our minds are occupied elsewhere. The price of transformation is eternal vigilance. Vigilance against being lulled back into conditioned beliefs and emotional/mental patterns that we think that we have 'overcome'. Illumination may well be a 'peak' in our development, but it isn't the end point, by any means. Those undergoing the initiation cycle in the West tend to find that many periodic death-rebirth experiences are necessary, as we reshuffle different 'bits' of the psyche with each occurrence. Yet the death-rebirth experience can bring about lasting benefits, including the alleviation of a wide variety of emotional, interpersonal, and psychosomatic problems that hitherto, have resisted orthodox treatment regimes.

I would postulate that the death-rebirth experience is an essential form of adaptive learning, as it is a powerful process of widening our perspectives on life, our perceptions of the world, and of each other. The illuminatory insight moves us toward a Holotropic perspective (i.e., of moving towards a whole) whereby new insights about self in relation to the universe, and how ideas and concepts synthesise together, can be startlingly perceived. At this kind of turning point in our lives, we can go beyond what we already know and begin to manifest new concepts and constructs. We are all capable of the vision—what we do to realise that vision is equally, in our hands.

GNOSIS

Related to the experience of Illumination is the term Gnosis, which can be read on different levels. First, Gnosis is that 'peak' experience of no-mind, one-pointedness or samadhi which is the high point of any route into magical trance. Second, Gnosis can be understood as *Knowledge of the Heart*—perceptions that are difficult to express in language, yet can be grasped and shared. This is the secret language of magic—to grasp the meaning you have to go through the experience first. Gnosis is not merely the act of understanding, it is understanding which impels you to act in a certain way. Thus as you work with magic, so magic works upon you. Such is the nature of Chaos.

Further Reading

Amookos, *Tantra Magick* (Mandrake of Oxford, 1990)
Angerford & Lea, *Thundersqueak* (TMTS, 1987)
Bey, Hakim, *T.A.Z.* (Autonomedia, 1991)
Burroughs, William, *Exterminator!* (Viking, 1973)
Burroughs, William, *The Adding Machine* (Calder, 1985)
Carroll, Peter J., *Liber Null & Psychonaut* (Weiser, 1987)
Carroll, Peter J., *Liber Kaos* (Weiser, 1992)
Carroll, Peter J., *PsyberMagick* (New Falcon Publications, 1997)
Crowley, Aleister, *The Book of Thoth* (Weiser, 1973)
Crowley, Aleister, *The Book of Lies* (Haydn Press, 1962)
Falorio, Linda, *The Shadow Tarot* (Headless Press, 1991)
Fries, Jan, *Visual Magick* (Mandrake of Oxford, 1992)
Fries, Jan, *Helrunar* (Mandrake of Oxford, 1993)
Gleick, J., *Chaos* (Cardinal, 1987)
Grant, Kenneth, *Nightside of Eden* (Skoob, 1994)
Hine, Phil, *Prime Chaos* (New Falcon Publications, 1999)
Hine, Phil, *The Pseudonomicon* (Dagon Productions, 1996)
Hofstadter, D., *Metamagical Themas* (Penguin, 1985)
Hurley, J. Finley, *Sorcery* (RKP, 1985)
Johnstone, K., *IMPRO* (Methuen, 1981)
Lee, D., *Magical Incenses* (R23, 1992)
Sherwin, Ray, *The Book of Results* (R23, 1992)
Spare, Austin O., *The Book of Pleasure* (93 Publishing, 1975)
Svoboda, Robert E., *Aghora* (Brotherhood of Life, 1986)
Starhawk, *Dreaming the Dark* (Unwin, 1990)
Walsh, R. N., *The Spirit of Shamanism* (Mandala, 1990)
Wilson, Steve, *Chaos Ritual* (Neptune, 1994)

New Falcon Publications

Invites You to Visit Our Website:
http://www.newfalcon.com

At the Falcon website you can:

- Browse the online catalog of all of our great titles
- Find out what's available and what's out of stock
- Get special discounts
- Order our titles through our secure online server
- Find products not available anywhere else including:
    - One of a kind and limited availability products
    - Special packages
    - Special pricing
- Get free gifts
- Join our email list for advance notice of New Releases and Special Offers
- Find out about book signings and author events
- Send email to our authors (including the elusive Dr. Christopher Hyatt!)
- Read excerpts of many of our titles
- Find links to our author's websites
- Discover links to other weird and wonderful sites
- And much, much more

Get online today at http://www.newfalcon.com